The Climbing Art

terature, poetry, and art for and about the spirit of climbing

Volume No. 28

Poudre Canyon Press
Bellvue, CO • Lincoln, NE

Cover: watercolor by John Svenson

ISBN: 1-881663-05-1

Printed in Canada

The Climbing Art

Editor: Scott Titterington
Contributing Editor: Ron Morrow
Circulation: Melissa Saathoff
Associate Editor: Christiana Langenberg
Business Manager: Ted Lannan
Publisher: Gary Gabelhouse

Editorial
P.O. Box 1378
Laporte, CO 80535
(970) 221-9210

Circulation & Advertising
5815 So. 58th Street
Lincoln, NE 68516
(800) 755-0024

The Climbing Art is published two times each year by Poudre Canyon Press, P.O. 1378, Laporte, CO 80535 (970) 221-9210. Second-class postage pending at Laporte, Colorado 80535. **Postmaster:** Please send address changes to The Climbing Art, P.O. Box 1378 Laporte, CO 80535

Manuscripts, photographs, poetry, artwork, and correspondence welcome. Send material to P.O. Box 1378, Laporte, CO 80535. Queries accepted, also. Please include a S.A.S.E.

Subscription rates are $18 for one year and $30 for two years for postal delivery in the United States. Add $10 per year for surface postage to Canada and $15 per year for surface postage to other foreign countries. All subscriptions payable in U.S. funds only. Please allow up to eight weeks for address changes or delivery of your first issue. Send subscription orders, address changes, and other correspondence to: The Climbing Art, 5815 South 58th Street, Lincoln, NE 68516.

Contents

No. 28

My Brother's Keeper

by James Michael Warren

Nobody climbed with Kane twice. Those who knew him told me not to climb with him. They said he was odd, had a loose screw, a bizarre sense of humor. They forecasted a rash of bad luck if we climbed together. But none of them wanted to break away from their jobs to climb the mountain, and the rainy season arrived in a month. I itched to climb and Kane's dance card was empty. I didn't care about his sense of humor. I just needed a climbing partner, someone to belay me on the steep sections of the mountain. I asked him to hook up with me. He agreed.

We flew into Katmandu, picked up our climbing permit, and caught the first plane to Lukhla. There we hired a Sirdar to guide us and a dozen porters to carry our gear to base camp at Mera La. I'd hired this Sirdar before and knew he didn't give a damn about climbing. But for a few extra rupees he'd keep his mouth shut if we decided to bag an extra peak, or climb a different route on our proposed peak.

The trek to base camp went without a hitch. We hiked for six days, gradually acclimatizing to the increasing elevation. None of the porters got sick or struck for higher wagers. No one stole our gear. I spent the time observing Kane, trying to figure him out.

I liked what I saw. Kane was strong. Standing six foot three and only twenty-three years old, he didn't know the word tired. While I hiked with a light daypack, he shouldered a pack weighing close to seventy pounds. I kept up with him only because he'd slow down when I lagged behind. And, he didn't talk much. Some guys have a habit of screwing up a climb by jabbering about the bullshit back home. I like a guy who knows how to keep quiet. Sometimes the success of a climb depends on everyone just shutting up, putting their heads down, and putting one foot in front of the other. Hell, I'd climb with Kane any day.

On the sixth day we climbed the Khare Glacier and arrived at Mera La feeling strong and well acclimatized. We set up base camp at seventeen thousand, a few feet beneath the col, paid the porters and told half of them to return in two weeks. Even with bad weather we could climb

Mera Peak in two weeks. Legally the Sirdar had to remain with us. But who would know if he sacked out in base camp while Kane and I climbed?

We rested in base camp for two days watching the weather and studying the mountain. Every afternoon the jet stream sprang up at about twenty thousand feet to push the clouds across the sky. The mountain grumbled with the rumbling of avalanches when the wind ripped against it. Our proposed route went along a knife edge ridge line, safe from avalanches.

While we rested, I had a chance to learn a little more about my climbing partner. He'd been climbing since his fifteenth year when he ran away from home. He loved the mountains. He said the icy slash of the wind in his face on the mountainside was a thousand times better than the heavy slap of his father's fist. He knew what to expect of the mountains and how to respect them. He said he climbed in harmony with the mountain. I liked his philosophy.

On the third day we started climbing before dawn. We planned to climb alpine style. The idea was to push up to nineteen thousand, set up a high camp below the jet stream, then summit the next day with a possible bivouac near the top. With perfect weather and no mishaps we knew we could be back in base camp on the fourth day.

Everything went according to plan the first day. We reached nineteen thousand by early afternoon, leveled a platform in the snow, and set up our tent. Kane fired up the stove and melted snow for tea while I sorted gear for our summit attempt. I decided to only take four ice screws, some runners and couple snow pickets along with the rope. The mountain appeared easier than I'd thought and Kane climbed as well as me. With less gear we'd have less weight and climb faster. I figured we might not have to bivouac if we climbed fast.

That afternoon we drank tea, ate soup, and dozed in our bags. Time passed slowly. A couple of times I tried joking with Kane. He didn't laugh. That's okay, I thought. He's focused on the climb and that's good. We wanted to be climbing shortly after midnight the next morning. I snuggled into my bag and tried to sleep.

It felt like I'd only been asleep for an instant when Kane gently shook me awake. "It's midnight," he said. "Let's get ready to climb."

Kane heated water while I searched for my headlamp then handed me a cup of warm tea and watched as I stuffed my bag into my pack. While I fumbled with the frozen laces of my boots he waited patiently. Finally we left the security of the tent and slowly climbed through darkness toward the ridge line. I followed behind.

We reached the ridge before dawn. The moon hung low on the horizon. The light from our headlamps danced on the snow. The ridge began wide but narrowed to a knife edge almost immediately. It rose at a sixty-degree angle. From this point on the climb became technical. Kane smiled. I felt like an amateur.

"Do you mind if I lead the first pitch?" he asked.

"No."

I handed him the ice screws and runners.

He climbed swiftly. His axe bit confidently into the ice. The points of his crampons barely scratched the surface as he climbed up the ridge. After half a rope length he placed his first piece of protection. At the end of the pitch he anchored then belayed while I climbed clumsily up to join him. The sun rose in the sky.

I peered up and knew I didn't want to lead the next pitch. It looked like difficult climbing. The ridge angled up at seventy degrees and continued for about five hundred feet before easing off.

"My head's pounding," I lied. "Must be the altitude. You

want to lead the next few pitches?"

"My pleasure," he grinned and started climbing.

I belayed and congratulated myself for asking Kane to hang with me on the mountain. I decided I made the right move when I ignored everyone's warnings about him. He climbed elegantly.

After a while the ridge widened and the angle eased off. The mountain rose in a pyramid before us. We stood on its summit shortly before noon. Kane took a picture of me then I took one of him. We ate a couple of Powerbars and savored the view from twenty-two thousand feet. Then we descended.

A breeze sprang up before we'd gone a hundred feet. Within minutes it grew to gale force. We anchored our ice axes in the snow and fell against the mountain. The wind tried to pry us off. Kane edged toward me.

"Can't go down in this," he yelled.

The wind snatched his words away.

"We'll have to dig a snow cave," he said.

He pointed to a buildup of snow below.

We inched down the mountain and burrowed into the mound of snow with our axes. The cave developed slowly. It took two hours to dig a hole large enough for both of us. We crawled in, away from the wind. I pulled out my bag and covered the entrance with my pack. Kane lit the stove to melt snow. I crawled into my bag and accidentally knocked over the pan of melting snow. The water soaked into Kane's bag. He quietly placed the pan back on the stove. He didn't say anything, but I saw he was pissed. I apologized. Silence filled the rest of the day while the wind howled outside.

The next morning the wind still blew. I cracked a couple jokes, but Kane was silent. Finally I shut up and waited for the wind to die off so we could climb down the mountain. That's when he spoke.

"Ever wonder what it's be like to kill someone?"

I swallowed, then shook my head.

Kane leaned back against the wall of the cave. "I could kill you and no one would ever know it."

"C'mon man, what're you talking about?" I pressed against the opposite wall.

"I could bury the pick of my axe in your fucking chest and there's nothing you could do about it," he smirked.

"You're joking!" I couldn't believe what I heard.

He picked up his ice axe. "I'd leave you in the cave and fill it with snow, then tell 'em you fell. They'd never find you."

"Stop it, Kane! You're scaring me"

"I can get off the mountain without you. You're just excess baggage."

I knew he was right. The entire climb I'd marveled at his effortless grace while I clumsily tried to keep up.

"Let's just get off this damn mountain when the wind dies down and go our separate ways," I moaned.

"You'd like that, wouldn't you?"

Outside the wind subsided. Kane tilted his head, listening. I pulled my pack away from the entrance and peered out. It was a beautiful crisp, blue-sky day.

"Let's forget this happened," I said, and started to load my pack.

He bent forward. I felt his breath rasp in my face.

"What do you think you're doing? You're not going anywhere," he sneered raising his axe.

An ice screw lay in the snow. I grabbed and jerked to the side when he lunged. The ice screw ripped across his throat, deep. His pick ripped into my sleeping bag. He dropped the axe and clutched his throat looking startled, not believing what just happened. His mouth opened and closed like a fish out of water but no sound emerged. The blood flowed easily, quickly soaking into his bag. In just a few seconds he drooped, then fell onto his side in the snow. I watched, horrified.

Kane was dead and I had killed him. I was stunned. I thought about trying to haul him down the mountain but decided I'd probably fall and die in the process. No one would believe me if I told them the truth. Why cart down the evidence that would convict me? Then I remembered what Kane said he had in store for me.

I left him in the cave and filled it with snow. I'd report that he fell on the descent. Maybe in a couple thousand years some one might find him. I hoped not in my lifetime.

The descent back to high camp took two days since I was by myself. On the most difficult sections of the mountain I rappelled off single ice screws. When I ran out I chopped bollards in the ice and rappelled off them. Several times I nearly fell. Many times I nearly gave up. When I reached the tent I lit the stove and melted snow. I drank it them melted more and drank that. Then I slept.

The next day I descended to base camp and told the Sirdar about the accident. He shook his head frowning and walked away mumbling. A week later the porters returned to carry the gear back to Lukhla. The Sirdar went ahead to report the accident to the authorities. I stayed with the porters.

Some friends met me at the airport when I landed in Los Angeles. They carried my gear out to their car and we drove to a nearby Mexican restaurant frequented by local climbers. We ate and drank beer. They listened intently while I recounted the trip and shook their heads sympathetically when I described Kane's fall. We reminisced about Kane. Everyone had a story to tell. They were all bizarre.

Then a guy walked over from a nearby table and said he'd been listening to our conversation. He'd climbed with Kane once himself and remembered an experience when the two of them were stuck in a snow cave for a couple days. Kane had gone silent and appeared moody those two days they waited out the storm. Then all of a sudden he started talking crazy about killing him and who would know? It ended with Kane lunging forward and suddenly grabbing him in a big bear hug. "Man, I was scared shitless," he laughed. "I thought for sure that ice axe was headed for my heart." I excused myself from the table. Suddenly I felt sick.

The Cost of Things

by Tracey Titterington

If Joe following Pete and Nan hadn't been treed by a brown bear awake early, a cubless mamma starving and pissed on the winding trail up to Grey Rock.

If Pete hadn't believed the news reports always as unreliable as the Front Range weather itself, if he would've instead slipped beyond contentment and noticed the creeping clouds growing gray squeaking barely above his Yeti sweat-shaped cap.

If Nan at the beginning of things hadn't run to the car back forth back for extra food water snacks.

If the three hadn't stopped, craving a breakfast of huge cinnamon sugar rush rolls, caffeined coffee at Vern's in LaPorte, then again stopped at the top after the bear and the satisfaction and the scenic hike with a Powerbar pause to look back over the shoulder to Fort Collins and Jeez, look how the Denver smog is penetrating, check it out, spreading thick into everything, yeah, then stopped to pitch their North Face tent camouflaged green gray within the wide sweeping green moose meadow and drop some gear.

If none of this had happened there would've been time.

If any one of the three would've trusted nature instinct, would've looked up slit eyes protected by shaded amber Vuarnets, purpled Frogskinned Oakley eyes, tipped way up past one belay on face, then another, three pitches, four, face steep 5.10a consistent, what were they thinking? 5.10 anyhow with a long no protection runout. If one had looked to the summit, beyond the shiny new slings and quad cams and stoppers and 'biners, even a few RP's, though what good could they be on this route? If they had searched beyond the gear and the moment to the goal top spiny scrub, they might've *seen.*

If any one of the three climbing would've looked down at tight, rubber-soled feet, rule number one for beginners, move the feet up not the weakling arms, small muscled, no huge leg quad sets. Feet, the feet, watch them. Always. If only they'd have looked down at those feet once, used those lessons, they'd have seen it: their skinny afternoon sun-sparked shadows stretching, catching storm dark.

By the time they noticed anything other than each body against rock, the sky was hissing black spit yellow split trouble.

shit shit shit

Why didn't we notice? yells Pete from belay stance three pitches up, three long lengths of rope, part way up 500 feet sheer rock face, another 5.10a long runout to go to lightning struck summit.

shit shit shit shit

We're in for it now.

What to do? Nan climbing third moves fast. Pete first, leading, Joe second on this pitch.

They could've sat it out, pause for one hour, two, impatient wet slick hours under overhang not big enough for three, one standing, or maybe rotate one then another human target into open ear-splitting thunder.

Or they could've climbed swift, move fast, scurry scamper, focus. To summit. Rush Off. Pray for the first time since grade school when belief was easy. No strikes. No rain. No damn 5.10 left. Time, our friend.

They could've done that, finished the climb.

Instead they said sacrifice the gear. At least Pete and Nan said it. Sacrifice it, Joe. Rappel, yeah, let's rap, man, Pete said. *Hurry.*

Now they move. Bomber Alien #4 wedged in crack. It ain't movin' nowhere, man, Joe says. Nan says, back it up anyhow. Backed up with Stopper #7. A new sling. Next time, we'll bring one or two old webbing slings, dammit.

shit shit shit

Joe bumming big time, $67 bucks plus tax down the tubes. Nan saying, We'll get it tomorrow. Come *on*!

If Joe wouldn't have hesitated, wouldn't have sniveled, if the new Black Diamond 10.5 rope with neon pink flecks in gray hadn't snagged on scrub at the top of the second pitch, Nan yanking it, hurry, faster, seconds wasted.

If lightning hadn't struck to the left of Joe going down first on the last pitch as he rapped quick, nearly down, if he would've noticed his hair, felt it stand, prickly under his hat.

If lightning piercing rock face hadn't struck inches from Joe, if it hadn't jagged into granite, through solid heart blast seconds of ground travel to Joe's sticky rubber-sheathed Boreal shoes, black with card player diamond heart club spade etched in neon green, no bluffing, pain beyond scrunched toes, zagging up torso, vertical out ears, tapping heart first.

If lightning hadn't happened then Joe wouldn't have had his heart stopped, wouldn't have blacked out then hung swinging limp only ten feet off ground, smelling sizzled and singed.

If Nan and Pete could hear, Pete through blown out ear drums, Nan's ears ringing telephone burst thrum, Hello? Hello?

If Nan, the least injured, could've rapped down, lowered Joe, lowered herself, to solid ground, then Pete down next after Nan off rappel, then the speed demon run down the narrow trail for help.

If Nan would've zigzagged down trail to rangers, rescuers, calling out troops, volunteers, help groups, if she hadn't tripped, flown on slimy rain slick log, falling, yelling shit, a litany, and bumped her rock head, cut temple, then blanked too.

If anyone had missed the friends. One day. Two. It's spring break Hurrah! breaking time.

Two days. Three.

If Ed, the hiker, and his wife, Liz, would've hiked on Wednesday instead of Friday, they'd have seen Joe limp, hanging, instead of hidden slumped behind the non-berried gooseberry bushes, the un-leaved poison ivy scrub.

If anyone, someone, would've heard Pete calling, heard his voice grow scratchy throaty to disappear raw rough one day into the hypothermic night, maybe, just maybe, help would've come on time.

Back in Quito

by Ron Morrow

With Ruccu Pinchincha and Cotopaxi behind us, we found ourselves back in Quito. Our next climb, Chimborazo, would be our last, but first an impromptu rest day was added to our agenda. Our small group, all of us from the Iowa Mountaineers, had hired an experienced guide from Colorado. He had patiently led our group of armchair and would-be alpinists up a series of Ecuadorian volcanoes, and the grateful novices, with some encouragement, were soon calling him "Papa Paul." When Papa said that his brood needed a rest day of shopping at the Indian market in the village of Cuenca, the kids obediently boarded a bus. I stayed behind.

Between climbs our group stayed in the heart of the El Centro section of Quito at the Hotel Casino Real Audiencia. When everyone else left, I slept in, then sauntered upstairs to the restaurant on the top floor to enjoy a large glass of cold, fresh-squeezed orange juice, a new Cuban cigar, and a good book. The book *Desperate People,* was an early attempt by Mowat.

The bustle of El Centro was seven floors below me. I love to explore a new city, alone on foot, walking past other lives, listening, peeking in, forming a disjointed collage that layers itself into an impression of a city. I planned to stretch the stiffness from Cotopaxi out of my legs by walking across town. Perhaps I would linger in the Parque Humboldt and then continue to the Hotel Colon where a lavish Sunday Brunch is served. After brunch I might browse through the English-language section in one of the many bookstores in the area. Quito, I had found, was a wonderfully literate city.

The Hotel Casino Real Annuncion is near the traffic circle where most of the city buses begin and end their routes. The side streets are full of shops and street vendors, and as the morning progresses a wall of people and a cacophony of hawkers and horns would fill the area. The city is alive, and I enjoy watching it from the terrace with its warm sun, cool shaded tiles, fluttering pigeons, metal chairs, and glass-topped tables. It was such a contrast with the picture that Mowat offered of the Canadian North.

Mowat wrote about the Innuit families who were camped near a new military base at Churchill in the Northwest Territories. The Eskimos were having a hard winter. They were hungry and in a dire condition. They assumed that the soldiers were traders and a source for help, but when they approached the military base with its elaborate equipment, they approached with trepidation and awe. The soldiers at first accepted their visitors with a sense of fascination, but as time passed the fascination eroded with familiarity that wore to annoyance as the soldiers, busy with their tasks, stepped back into their own unspoken community: the things that made them what they were and those who were not, not. The Eskimos did not know how to ask for the simple things they needed. The soldiers never realized the pain and desperation of the people living next door to them. They would have helped gladly, but they had no idea that the children were starving to death. For a moment the starkness of that image shocked me, and that horror would have lingered if *Desperate People* had been the first Mowat that I had read. It was not. Mowat was guilty of his typical emotional excesses. I thought of the British tourist in E.M. Forester's *Passage to India.* Forester handles these things so much better than Mowat. Still, the image of dead children would be a difficult tool for a writer to use effectively.

I finished my orange juice, stuck the book into my back pocket—I never go anywhere without a book—and waded out into the crowded city. What a city. Quito rests in the Avenida de Volcanes, which offers a distant backdrop of shimmering summits that seem to float in the blue sky. Close by is the lavish Irish Green of Ruccu and Guanga Pichinchas. Farmers cultivate the steep mountain sides in terraced fields. It looks like a picture from *The Hobbit.* The town itself consists of buildings covered in stucco of muted tan or whitewashed with roofs of red tile or tin that roar in the heavy rain. The streets are steep and narrow and paved with brick and cobblestone and they are brimming with townspeople and Indians in their brightly colored traditional dress. Men carry enormous loads strapped to their backs. There are thirty-six cathedrals, all of them splendid. Their alters and naves are plated with gold.

I was well acclimated to the city's 9,800-foot elevation and was becoming adroit at dodging through the crowded streets. Within an hour I was in the grassy quiet of the Parque Humboldt. Couples strolled the paths while children chased each other around the monument to the German geographer Humboldt. A clacking sound followed by male laughter announced a Bocce Ball game chasing itself across the grass. Bets were made, and sucres were nervously folded and unfolded then passed from hand to hand. The laughter was tense.

Across the street from the park was the Hotel Colon. The hotel was luxurious, and its modern lines were accented with Christmas lights and decorations. I had come for the lavish Sunday brunch.

On the sidewalk, next to the hotel's entrance, a street vendor, a young woman, was selling oil paintings. The pictures were typical tourist fare: dark silhouettes of mountains, villages, and Christmas scenes. It would have been easy to ignore her, but in the corner of the stall someone had stuck in a child's drawing of Quito. In it green hills towered above a child's cartoon of El Centro. A military band played in the park while overhead black V's representing seagulls went "Peep, Peep, Peep" in a cartoonist bubble, and of course, near the top of the paper shimmered El Altar, Chimborazo, and Cotopaxi. The child's eye was true. I caught myself bent over the drawing examining the detail. That caught the woman's attention.

"That is cute," I caught myself with a smile after speaking English.

She picked up the picture and examined it herself. She stared at it as if she had really not noticed it before, and perhaps she had not. Then she answered my smile with a smile and a nod and put the picture behind her, face down.

Probably it was put there by the eager young artist and, of course, was not for sale. But she did have a poster that I wanted. It was the same poster that I saw hanging in a friend's apartment the year before. The poster was two photographs. On the left was a dark silhouette of a climber pushing to the top of the final steep pyramid of Cotopaxi. On the right was a picture of a climber ascending above the Red Wall of Chimborazo. Names and elevations were printed on the bottom. It offered good profiles of both peaks, and I could not resist.

"Que cuesta es ese?"

"Seven dollars and ninety-five cents."

The English startled me, and I took real notice of the woman for the first time. Unkempt is the first thing to say about her. She was pretty, maybe twenty-six or twenty-seven, thin and nervous, and unkempt not in the deliberate way that is occasionally the style but in a self-effacing destructive way, and perhaps that is deliberate, after all.

"You blend in well. Caught me off guard."

She was an American.

"I've been here a while."

"Where are you from?"

"Chicago."

"Really, I am from Gary Indiana...but normally I do not admit that."

She looked at me.

"Why not?"

"Would you? It is so barren."

She pointed to the cheap tourist paintings.

"Would you like one of these done on brushed velvet? It can be arranged. Actually I am from Elgin...a small town outside of Chicago."

"Really? When I think about that part of Illinois, I think about maple trees and huge, old wooden houses, a homey-type of place."

"It could be. This poster is very popular with climbers."

"Yes," I admitted. "It is hard to resist, a good reminder and of course a good way to guide a conversation, in a modest way of course."

"Oh yes, of course," she laughed.

"In fact, I want four of them."

"Not for over the fireplace, I hope."

"Well no but maybe over mom's. The only American dollars that I have are all in large denominations."

"I cannot make change in dollars, but we have a great exchange rate on sucres."

"That is okay. I am going to have brunch here at the hotel. I will get change there and come back afterwards. Is the food good there?"

"Oh yes it is very good, but it is very expensive."

"I read that it was only six or seven dollars."

"No, it is eight, I think."

"Well, I guess that I can manage that. After all I am a Yankee Tourista."

We spoke for some time. Her wit was quick and kept skirting the border of being sardonic. She had an outsider's detachment that offered clinical observations of a world occupied by denizens who could have resided in the best of Balzac's novels.

Speaking with her was very pleasant and, I caught myself blurting out, "Can you get away?"

She look startled.

"I mean for lunch, I mean brunch."

She hesitated a moment to consider the suggestion then swept her hand over her little stall then shrugged that off and said, "Actually, I would like that, if..."

She gave a nervous glance toward the park and shrugged. The Bocce Ball game was over, the players gone. She panned the street and focused on one of the players. He had a fist full of sucres, and he in turn surveyed us with a proprietary air. He approached and said something to her. Was he speaking to an employee? A lover? The man was old enough to be her father. The relationship, at first glance, did not look healthy.

When he looked away, she waved me away with a nervous gesture and said, "Well, thank you."

I answered quickly, "Well sure, I guess I better go make that phone call now. Thanks."

I turned to go, but behind me I could hear her speaking to him. I caught something about "...taza de cafe..." and so I lingered in the lobby. She greeted me with a smile and a toss of her hair. She gestured back toward the old man as if she wanted to dismiss him, so I did not ask. I wanted to ask.

Down the hall that led to the dining room, folding table after folding table was laden with exotic foods. We served ourselves, tasting small portions of several dishes. She identified and explained each one for me.

"I walked all of the way down here. My hotel is clear across town. I am famished."

She admonished me not to be shy.

"This is a luxury for me," she said. "I plan to enjoy it fully."

We found a vacant table. The food was wonderful. I brought up the topic of Quito. She was very knowledgeable. I found myself asking her if she had ever read Edward Whymper's *Travels Among The Volcanoes of the Equator*. She gave me a patient smile that made me realize how foolish the question was. The obscure book is over 100 years old and of interest only to mountaineers and not too many of them. Nevertheless, I found myself discussing it. I carried on and on about why he sailed so far to climb in Ecuador, about his triumph and tragedy on the Matterhorn, and of course his more famous book *Travels Among The Alps*. I had been thinking about Whymper all day. I felt like him: the outsider traveling in Ecuador and observing a new different culture. I generally agreed with his assessment of Ecuador. The novelty of it is very interesting, but with more familiarity it is more than wanting. I feel that way about most cultures, not with any animosity. In my heart, I have the same thought repeated, the type of thought that floats to the surface just before sleep or when I am very tired, the thought that before it is all said and done 98 percent of the people that you meet really are not worth knowing, but this thin woman with the wild hair had a smile and a sarcastic wit. Her story, whatever it was, had to be interesting.

"What?" Her voice focused me.

"You said that you were going to call."

"Oh, I just wanted to distance that...your friend out there."

"Him, Oh." She looked down. "I thought that maybe you were going to call the States."

"Well, I had thought about it," I lied.

Who would I call? I guess that I could have checked my answering service.

"You can do that from here?"

"What, oh I had read that this hotel has operators downstairs who take care of that. You can just pay them directly. That is what the guide books say."

"I did not know that." She looked very tense and kept busy rearranging her silverware, picking up a water glass and setting it down. "Family?" And she cleared her throat.

"No."

"No, you do not have any?"

"No, yes...I mean that I am something of the black sheep. We have not spoken in several years."

"I can relate to that," she laughed. "If you don't tell me your story, I won't tell you mine."

"If you insist."

Her humor was contagious, and I found myself joining in her laughter.

She was silent for a moment then said, "Well you know what it is like when men are estranged from their families. They are always young. They act as if they really relish the experience you know with all of the emotional excesses and the posturing and the 'just looking fer me pap' attitude. When all along the things that caused the estrangement were really insignificant."

I was at a loss for words. Should her prattle be dismissed as nervousness? It was irritating to hear so casual a dismissal for what to many men is a painful loss.

She realized her mistake, I think, and continued after a pause. "Well I am not close to my family either."

"Oh," I was still at a loss.

Brightly, "Well, have you been to Ambato yet?"

We were over the hard spot.

"That is where we are going in the morning. We will climb Chimborazo and then spend a couple of days at the hot springs in Ambato. Do you like Ambato? I have read quite a bit about it and all of what I have read has been good."

She looked wistful, "No, I have not made it over there yet, but I want to. It is hard to get away."

Again I was wondering about the old man. Again, I did not ask, but I had a sense that something was wrong.

"How many of you are there?" she abruptly changed the subject again.

"Eight of us, all from Iowa."

"How much do you think that it will cost?"

"Oh it is a package deal. The airfare was the worst of it."

"No, the telephone."

"What?" I couldn't guess the antecedent. Then I remembered, "Oh yes, the phone, I really do not know. It should be easy enough to find out. That is what is so nice about this hotel. They will do everything for you."

She looked up with an incredulous look on her face.

I was beginning to feel some incredulity myself. If it was so important to her, then why had she never checked it out? She spoke Spanish.

"If you'd like we could walk down there and ask."

"Would you mind?"

"No, of course not, but let us eat first."

"Fine, thank you," she said in a timid whisper.

The meal was as good as the books had promised. Afterwards

we found our way down to the basement of the hotel. Two operators, both polyglots, direct calls to the hotel and also arrange calls to foreign countries for guests and tourists. It was an easy arrangement. Why my guest never made the call herself, I do not know, but it looked as if she was going to now. She spoke in rapid Spanish with one of the operators. Then reading from a crumpled piece of paper, she gave her a number. The operator pointed to a bank of chairs where we waited for some time for the call to go through. When it did, the operator pointed to one of the soundproof booths, and my nervous companion disappeared inside it. She was gone but a few minutes. She returned flush but calm. She smiled at me and gave me a brief hug and let her lips brush against my cheek while she was passing.

"Thank you, that was very difficult."

She went to the operator to pay. The call was expensive, and I offered to help. She insisted, no, and she dug through the disarray of her purse and then dug through it again. Finally she unfolded enough sucres to cover the bill and was given a small handful of coins as change.

She told me, oddly with a smile, and in an almost matter-of-fact voice, "My father has died."

I started to say that I was sorry to hear that, but I realized that she was not. All that I could manage was a questioning, "Oh?"

She told me that her mother was to call back in an hour or so and that she would wait there for the call. She thanked me for the brunch. Then there was not much left for me to do except to leave.

"Well, good then I think that I will go and see the museum that you recommended." And I turned to go.

She rushed up to me and again gave me a brief kiss. "Thanks."

As she hugged me, I felt her small breast pressing against me. I told her the name of my hotel in case she needed any help, and then I kissed her. As I went up the hall I thought of lines from T.S. Eliot.

Back on the street I saw her employer hawking the paintings. If she was the kiss of April, he would be the last gaps of winter. He could have been her father. He leered. His pallor was unhealthy, his dress shabby. A beret was cocked over his stringy hair. After a short while in the museum, I admitted to myself that I was not in the mood for it, and within an hour I found myself back in the park across from the hotel. I took out my book. Mowat was still speaking about the starvation deaths of the children and again about how the well-intentioned soldiers who lived so close by were blind to their suffering. He does not make a compelling argument that the society that created the soldiers intentionally blinded them to the needs of others, an act that would have some moral relevance. I thought about Hume and the relationship between agency and morality. Where was the agency here? Mowat was beginning to irritate me again. His prattle made me think about Hegel's classifications, specifically about the people who lived in the realm of the heart. Starving children were irrelevant.

It was getting cold. I had lost myself in the book, and it was late in the afternoon. I glanced as the Hotel Colon. She was not there, so I started my weary walk back to my room. If I was lucky, I could grab a small nosh and then curl up with another book before my climbing companions returned from their shopping spree.

I was not to be so lucky. Several of them were lounging in the lobby trying to make points with tidbits of knowledge gleaned out of guidebooks and insisting that I admire the souvenirs they had purchased. More were in the restaurant. Two were drunk and loud. I listened to their excitement and to their descriptions of the trip and only wondered about the poverty of their language. After a small meal I escaped.

I tried to read but found myself slightly depressed. I was torturing myself with past mistakes. This one was about a woman that I had dated a couple of times several years ago. She had sneered on her way out and had said that I lived in the smallest house in Ames, Iowa. Then she slammed the door.

I did manage to finish reading the Mowat that I had started. That was when my friend from brunch called. She was in the lobby and asked if she could see me. I went down.

She had thrown a frayed serape over her cotton blouse. A suitcase and a bulging backpack were at her feet and a little boy was at her side.

"Hi."

"Hello."

"My mother arranged airfare for us. We are going back to Elgin."

I looked at her face expecting but not finding any signs of edema or ecchymosis or any other signs of violence. If anything she looked relaxed and happy.

"Well good for you." I asked the child, "Have you ever been on an airplane before?"

He was shy and did not answer.

"This is my son, Raúl."

"Hi Raúl."

He was an olive-skinned boy with wavy black hair and long eyelashes. His jeans were torn at the knees and his tennis shoes were worn and dirty. He clutched a Teddy bear in his arms.

"You're going to need a good coat in Illinois you know."

Still he was shy. His mother hugged him to her. I knew that there were only two planes that left for Guayaquil and then Miami each day. One left mid-morning, the other in the afternoon. I recalled that she had trouble covering the phone call that had set all of this into motion. And I suspected that there might not be money for food, taxis, or a place to stay the night. If they waited at the airport, would he come looking for them? I did not ask.

Instead I shrugged and commented to the mother, "Traveling light?"

"Oh yes, the dream of the sixties, but it loses it appeal when you are pushing thirty."

So I had guessed her age correctly.

"Did you get a chance to eat? Are you hungry? May I buy you dinner?"

This time she was shy. "Oh, I don't know."

So I turned to the child, "Raúl tiene más hambre? Quiere helado choclate?"

"Oh yes please," he answered in good English.

"Well, my young sir, there is a restaurant on the top of this hotel. You can see the whole city from there, and they serve an excellent chocolate ice cream."

The child smiled and grabbed my hand.

"Well I guess that we eat," I laughed.

She answered for him, "I guess so."

On the way upstairs I tucked their parcels in my room. Raúl went ahead and swaggered into the restaurant as if he owned the place. I tried to order a meal for him, but ice cream had been promised and ice cream was expected. I had much to learn about children. His mother ate light, and I only had a cup of coffee. The thin child ate the treat as if he had been starving. I took delight in ordering him a second dish.

The very way that his mother looked at him made her love appear obvious. And I caught myself grinning and nodding my head. To a casual observer we probably looked like a happy little family. That was okay. After he finished his ice cream, Raúl jumped from his chair and grabbed his bear and my hand and led us to the balcony railing. He squeezed two of my fingers in one of his hands while holding onto the railing with the other. He surveyed the city with wide eyes, then let go of my fingers to point at something. Speaking excited Spanish he turned to look for his mother.

"Mom," he called, and she joined us.

They spoke Spanish. I listened. These things were new to me.

Time passed quickly, and we found ourselves sitting in chairs sipping coffee. The child, Raúl, sat on his mother's lap fighting sleep.

"Your kid is tired."

"Yes, it is way past his bed time. We had better leave."

"To the airport?"

"It will do," she admitted.

"Climbers do have sleeping bags."

"No, we could not do that to you. We owe you too much as it is."

"What?"

"The phone call," she insisted.

"What about the phone call, and what is it that you would be doing to me?"

"Well, you know."

"No, I do not have the slightest idea."

She pressed the child to her but made no reply.

"Well," I continued, "I would worry."

"This is Ecuador. Quito has almost no crime."

"It does not take much crime. Besides your bags are already in my room. Y'know."

She consented with a simple, "Let's go then."

I scooped up the child. He squealed with laughter and hopped out of my arms and ran down the hall. We followed. When we got to my room, Raúl's curiosity led him straight to the climbing equipment that was laid out for Chimborazo. I unlooped the ice ax and let him hold it. Then he wanted to see the crampons. I took off the shields and let him rub his fingers over the points. Then I unraveled the straps and pressed one onto the base of a boot. He was fascinated. Over his mothers protest, we got out a rope and a set of Jumars. Before long he was clumping around the room in my boots. He had my ice ax in his hands and my helmet riding over his eyes. He was delightful.

His mother finally prevailed and was able to get him into bed. Then she dug out another stuffed animal and two books from his backpack. The four of them, mother, son, bear, and stuffed animal hunkered down with their books. She read in a musical tone and soon he was asleep. Then she joined me at the window, and I put down the book I was pretending to read.

"That wasn't so tough," I teased.

"No," she admitted, "I have always been lucky in that department, and he is finally getting to the age where he does not need constant supervision."

"I really do not know much about children," I had to admit. "I am an only child."

"I was in the same boat when Raúl was born. Before that I felt like a competent adult then I was a parent and overnight reduced to feeling about as competent as a sixteen-year-old kid. I wanted to call my mother for advice, at least six or seven times a day. I didn't but I certainly wanted to."

"Do you have any family down here."

"No, no, I have been how did you put it...estranged."

I shrugged and said nothing.

She continued, "It does seem odd to go home at my age. My poor mother never even knew that she was a grandmother until this afternoon.

"Oh, what did she say?"

"She said, 'OH!,'" my friend laughed. "That was not exactly what I expected, but she did add that she would kill the fatted calf and prepare a feast and all of the biblical stuff. You know pallet on the floor to boot, actually I think that she was delighted, very happy."

We were silent for a while and then the silence was broken by the noise from the street below our window. Inadvertently, I changed the subject to Quito. We spoke awhile longer, then she left me to lie down beside her beautiful child. I tried to read but could not lose myself. I paced, watched the street from the window, and paced again. I let myself out quietly and paced to the restaurant upstairs. For some time I stood watching the people below. I was not thinking anything. I was not feeling anything. I paced.

When I returned to the room, I found the mother protecting the young child with her arms. He slept peacefully. I watched them for a while, then unrolled my sleeping bag and tried to do the same. Insomnia was with me yet again, but I was finally able to sleep. There was one dream. I was in a small house peering out of a small window at my son asleep under a tree. And I thought about sitting beside him and reading stories to him, stories about little girls and spiders, stories about a mouse and a tiny canoe, and a story about a frog and a motor car. And I would wait for him to grow older and then give him the gift of Jules Verne and Captain Nemo. I would help him send off for catalogues from the Edmund Scientific Company and watch him save his allowance to buy beakers, stoppers, and bottles of colored chemicals. We would plan for science projects at school, canoe trips in Minnesota, and backpacking trips through the canyons of Southern Utah.

I was awakened by a soft rapping on my door. It was my wake up call. Breakfast was waiting for us and then the bus to Ambato. I left a short note and some cash, then I left. The next night would be spent in the *refugio* at the base of Chimborazo. That would be a new volume and I would be present in that new circumstance. The things before it could be closed and put away on a shelf.

The climb of Chimborazo was wonderful. My one regret was that we avoided the Whymper Route that I had read so much about. Instead of following his lead, we spent a day acclimating and then went up, skirted the red wall, turned left and headed straight for the summit. Still I was able to see his route in its entirety, and I was eager to compare our reality with his book. The summit was my highest.

After the climb we spent two days relaxing in the hot springs of Baños. Then we returned to Ambato for market day. Then we were back in Quito. Our little family split into smaller groups. Couples paired and left, some to tour the Galapagos Islands, some to canoe stretches of the Amazon River, and others to travel to Miami, to Chicago, and finally back to Iowa. I kicked around town for a day or two, and yes, foolishly I did look for her, but she was gone.

Another Breakfast at the Sportsman's Cafe

by Robert Walton

I spend hours, dozens of lowland winter hours, ponder ing guide books. I dream. I imagine. I try to crystallize the mysteries in the words into mountain realities. But mountain realities are found in the mountains.

This is an abyss. This is a precipice on top of an abyss. Arc Pass?

Below me, several hundred feet of steep talus end above black cliffs. A gulf of clear, sunny air falls away from these cliffs to Consultation Lake 1,800 feet farther down.

Seeking a better view, I hop lightly atop a truck-sized boulder. It slides several inches toward the lake. A nova-burst of adrenaline takes me soaring back toward solid ground. I tumble, roll, sprawl, sneeze in a cloud of dust.

Lincoln, leaning on his pack, smiles at me. Bonzo, all one hundred and forty golden pounds of him, pants and dog-grins at me. My stupidity has always amused my partners, especially Bonzo. I often feel he watches me to see what incomprehensible but humorous thing I will do next.

A long eastward traverse toward the end of the cliff band seems possible. I look at it and shrug. Lincoln nods his ascent. Bonzo curls his tongue in a laconic arc.

I look again for signs of a path. Nothing. We'd already come over the top of Langley and spent a joyous time exploring the Miter Basin. Most of our travel had been nowhere near a trail, but I would sure like to see some sign of previous passage now.

I step down. Dirt and shattered rock swallow me up to my calves. I wade into a tilted wasteland. I try to stay above the most delicately poised monster blocks. Lincoln stays twenty meters back. Bonzo—no dummy, he—takes a path somewhat above ours. Sweat, work, slide, sweat, halfway.

It is here, midway, that mountain horror sticks cold claws through my shell of concentration. It's happened to me before, as it has to all climbers, and the moments are priceless learning experiences—in retrospect. My personal highlights of self-doubt: Tuolumne, Pywiack, first time on the Dike Route, above the crux, twenty feet from the next bolt; Palisades, top of the U-Notch, front-pointing on ice we hadn't expected, forty feet above a #5 stopper, manky; the Pinnacles, Balconies, third pitch of Shake and Bake, three moves from Higgins' amazing bolt.

Now, Arc Pass—2nd class, my God!—And I'm again ready to pee in my socks. Everything is ready to slide off and take the shortcut to the lake. Everything. I cannot take another step.

Such moments pass.

I slump onto solid rock. Lincoln stumbles in after me. Bonzo, the first to reach terra firma, stares reproachfully at both of us. Why have we put a good dog like him through such a beastly experience? Good question.

Heart rate down, breathing less than frantic, nerves healing, confidence rising, I step down on the top of a talus fan that does not end in cliffs. It collapses. I become the centerpiece of my very own rock slide. After thirty feet, the buildup of dirt and stones in front of me brings me to a dusty halt.

Lincoln, watching my antics from the verge of a steep snow gully, inquires about my health. I tell him I'm fine and assure him that I'm going the right way. He smiles, waves and starts boot-skiing down the forty-degree snow. Bonzo follows him. My route-finding skills have always inspired confidence in my partners.

I continue my avalanche act for several hundred yards. Lincoln parallels me, cutting bold, elegant Z's in the hard snow. Bonzo, built in crampons working nicely, takes a direct route down the snow. He nearly loses it once, but ends up taking a nap at the bottom while I'm still raising clouds of dust.

Pretty soon, a vast jumble of loosely piled boulders ends my downward progress. Lincoln and Bonzo are eighty feet below me on easy snow. Time to quit rock-hopping.

It's spooky getting to that snow. All those boulders seem poised to fall. I slip, caress, claw, pray, launch! A feet-in-the-air, snow-in-my-underpants glissade ensues—a classic Waldo Walton glissade.

Cleaning snow out of my ears with tip of my little finger, I notice Bonzo. He's panting patiently and eyeing me with mild disapproval. He obviously considers my recent performance to be well below group standard on snow.

Drained, both physically and emotionally, we eventually flop down in a sandy-bottomed cleft among boulders near Consultation's outlet. Our descent has taken three hours. We eat. We drink. We rest. We sweat.

We sweat a great deal. It's ungodly hot in that cleft. Bestirring ourselves, we erect a sunshade—my tarp strung across the gap between a couple of rocks. Bonzo plants himself in the deepest shade the tarp affords as Lincoln ties the last knot. It's a small tarp, a limited patch of shade. Bonzo tilts his head to an imperial angle and regards us with challenging majesty. If Lincoln and I wish to cuddle up to a large, golden dog and rest in the fringes of the shade, it will be permitted. Thanks, Bonzo. Good dog.

Lincoln and I look at each other. We both turn and look up at Whitney's towers. We look back at each other. He shrugs. I shrug. It's only 2:30. We've never done it by the trail. Besides, it's there.

Lincoln's cheery voice rouses me. I roll over. Aches shout up from my knees to remind me that we came down from Whitney in yesterevening's dusk. Interestingly enough, we were nearly killed on the way up. Halfway to Trailcrest, among the endless switchbacks, we encountered rock fall—half a dozen basketballs and a convoy of smaller ones. They rushed and crushed the trail some five meters or so in front of us. Killed on the trail? It does go with being scared to death on a Class II pass.

Lincoln and I rightly suspected that we had nearly been the victims of careless trundling. A few moments of fearful ducking and high-altitude sprinting brought us up a switchback and in view of a trail crew. They were slightly—very slightly—chagrined to see us appear. No lookout. No warning shout. Just heave-ho.

We said unkind things to them. They responded that they had not expected hikers to be coming up the trail this late in the afternoon. Obviously. We said further unkind things to them. They became surly. We departed in anger.

The summit calmed me. Sunlit and vast, it seems more like a remote shoreline than a mountaintop. I've been there a number of times and it always affects me in the same way. Except for Russell, other mountains are low or on the horizon. Whitney is a world unto itself, self-contained, remote.

Knees be damned. I paw my way up out of my bag and discover that Lincoln isn't talking to me. Two sturdy men in shorts, huge packs perched lightly on their shoulders, stand in the middle of our little bay. They radiate purpose, energy, and neatness. Our possessions are scattered like trash across the landscape. I feel frowzy and embarrassed.

The older man asks, "Are you the guys who came down Arc yesterday?"

We are indeed.

"Which one of you skied down the couloir?"

Lincoln smiles.

"That was a bold thing to do."

They have obviously Just descended Arc Pass—before

breakfast. I'm impressed.

The younger man—deeply tanned and possessed of huge calf muscles—mutters, "It was a bear. What a bear!"

His partner then inquires, "Where's the trail?"

Lincoln and I stare blankly at each other. At last I motion vaguely to the northeast. We have NOT yet had our coffee, after all.

We have been proven both messy and dumb. The two mountain men have no more time for us. Cheerful and unflustered, they bid us good-bye and disappear down the stream which flows Just to the east of our dell.

Before the young man's intimidating calves wink out of sight, I hear him say once again, "What a bear!"

A bruin indeed, old Arc. Or is he referring to Bonzo?

Well—we have no choice after this encounter but to get our act together. We do. After coffee.

We launch ourselves down the way our morning acquaintances took and intercept the trail. We have no desire to see that tent suburb of LA. up by the bathrooms again.

Down.

Fast.

But not as fast as I'd planned. An attractive young woman spots Bonzo and uses him as a good excuse to take a break from her upward grind. Scruffy graybeards such as Lincoln and I do not inspire friendly conversation in attractive young ladies. Bonzo does. And a great deal more.

She pats him, cuddles him, and coos over him to such an extent that even his great patience is strained. It's obvious in the ironical twist of his lip as he pants.

Get used to it, Pal.

This performance is repeated by at least a dozen more beautiful, athletic, young women. On the best day of the greenest-salad days of my youth I did not receive one tenth of the enthusiastic female affection he has been accorded in less than an hour. It's not fair. Is my nose not long enough? Not black enough?

We drag Bonzo out of the clutches of yet another admirer and head down the last big drop to Whitney Portal. What a hot piece of tilted desert it is! That last mile or so of sage and white dust raises my first blister of the trip. Damn, after all those miles.

As I at last plunge into the Portal's shade, I know that only beer—COLD beer—will insure my survival until sunset. I beeline to the store and acquire a six-pack of Miller's. My mind is now at rest.

Lincoln grins and shakes his head tolerantly at the single-mlndedness of my beer thirst. We clump on to the car. My Honda seems an alien contrivance after a week on foot. We pile our backpacks in—no easy task, considering Bonzo requires more than half of the back seat—and go down to site 44. Lincoln and I have occupied site 44 before and found it to be the best car-camping site in our experience—big, shaded and totally isolated. It's occupied, but the occupants are leaving. We sit down to await their departure.

Papa, a man some ten or twelve years younger than I; directs wife and blond children to police the camp. This they do twice during the ensuing two hours. We found later that they were not cleaning up litter, (we picked up much stray paper and trash) but were making sure they'd misplaced none of their possessions—pins, for instance. Papa meanwhile begins to brush off the tent trailer with a toothbrush. He does this twice to make sure he's not missed a spot. Other more mysterious packings and foldings take place.

Lincoln and I, our minds boggling, continue to peer at them. They all gather around the tent trailer and proceed to fold it down like Charles Boyer folding Greta Garbo's silk negligee.

Papa gets in the red Cherokee and starts it up.

Lincoln and I stir.

Too soon. Too soon. Too soon

Papa turns everyone out for one more search of the camp. At last they pile in and hit the road.

Lincoln and I remain seated for a moment of silence. We know we have witnessed something unique. This whole three-hour performance has been executed without verbal communication. Like a ritual. Amen.

We rise, walk into camp, and drop our sleeping bags. Moved in.

After retrieving Lincoln's truck from Horseshoe Meadow, visiting the market in Lone Pine, and journeying back up the Portal hill, we settle down in camp and begin to relax. Supper is sometime in the future. A nap is at hand. Roll my frumpy gray sweater into a pillow. Settle back on pine needles. Lazy-gaze up at drifting silver clouds of Portal cliffs. Eyelids slip down easy as night falling.

Something is moving. Something purple is moving toward me. I tilt my head, try to focus. A man, elderly and husky, is approaching. He has the official and proprietary air of a campground host and is not purple.

My eyes widen. A true apparition is on this man's heels: wide, bloated, warty, purple—a 300-pound purple toad? No. The toad is a lady, of sorts. Her dress is a circus tent of a purple nu-mu, a garment I'd long though to be outlawed by civilized societies.

The host opens his mouth to greet us, but purple mu-mu speaks (perhaps "brays" would be a better word) first.

"There are four in our party. WE have lots of equipment and out site is rather CRAMPED."

Yes.

"There are TWO in YOUR party and you have little equipment."

Yes.

"Your site is much roomier, more secluded and nicer

than OURS."

Yes.

"It seems only fair that we exchange sites. RIGHT NOW, before we unpack all our gear."

Lincoln and I peer at each other in wonder.

"WELL???"

Well, no.

"NO?"

No.

Mu-mu's eyes do a tremendous toad-pop. Her mouth claps shut. She whirls—a not unimpressive feat of athleticism—and huffs off. The host, looking more than a little pained, shrugs, turns, and follows her.

Lincoln and I ponder this experience in silence. Indeed what words would suffice? I soon rise and get us both a beer. This seems the only rational response to our encounter with purple mu-mu.

Deep, deeper in a drowsy afternoon, my eyelids again drift south. Sunlight peeks and pokes beneath our thick roof of fir needles. The stream, just past my right shoulder, takes a few steep steps in its long walk to the desert. Purple intrudes on my peripheral vision.

I have to look.

Yes, it's mu-mu. She's walking her dog, a nasty-looking black Chow, on the path by the stream. The low-browed brute pulls bullishly on its leash. To no avail. Mu-mu has it vastly outweighed. Bonzo sniffs, raises his eyes heavenward in an eloquent gesture of disdain at sharing doghood with such a creature and buries his nose under his tail.

Mu-mu decides to cross the swift-rushing but shallow stream. Midway, doubt assails her. The Chow suddenly lunges for the bank. Mu-mu brays, teeters, falls.

She falls like a toddler, butt first. Her rump obliterates a shallow pool. The stream rears up in crushed agony behind her and pours liquid ice down the back of her blighted dress. Her mouth makes repeated beached trout gasping motions, but no sounds come out. Her eyes are slightly more popped out than usual.

Lincoln and I sit frozen in indecision. Does she need help? Does the stream? I rise and move tentatively to the rescue.

Before I can take my third step, she lurches to her feet, utters a howl of rage and plops down on the bank. I judge the danger has passed and return to my seat.

Glaring at us all the while, she lets the Chow pull her soggily up the bank and into the undergrowth. Lincoln and I look at each other, nod. Time for another beer.

The evening is long and peaceful.

We spend the morning's early hours watching sun light progress down white cliffs. We tacitly abandon our intention of taking another crack at Lone Pine Peak's North Ridge: too much mountain for our mood, too hot—again—too hot. We decide instead to try out my new East Side climber's guide.

Bushwhack upwards for twenty minutes or so. A wall stops us, a wall that looks vaguely like several of the guide's illustration. Progress!

We don shoes, harnesses, and get out the rack. The rack—quite brilliantly, I've left most of my stuff at home. This is my mountaineering gear: wired stoppers and a few big hexes, no Friends, no TCUs. Hell, it's only one pitch. It's only 5.8 if we've got the right climb. Hell.

Well, hell, I'm ninety feet out. I'm also definitely getting older. That first thirty feet—lie back up a steep crack, pull up into a humping mantle onto a pointed block — pooped me.

Humping mantle? Must be a bad day. Also, I've reached an awkward spot and the end of my year simultaneously.

I check my gear sling again, just in case. My three big

hexes are hanging around like fat nerds at the end of a high school dance. They're embarrassed to be so useless, but they've got no place else to go.

The previously enjoyable crack has turned dirty, rounded, rotten, and there is a dying cactus in the way. I ponder this little problem. As I do so, I come off. There must have been some grit on the edge where I planted my right foot. Anyway, the down elevator takes me.

Fear? I can't figure it out. Sometimes fear is a whale that swallows me whole. It gobbled me up on Arc Pass. This time—as I actually dangled at the end of my 10mm rope—chagrin, embarrassment and anger fill me. Five feet below my last stopper, I curse and punch the innocent, unresisting air.

Lincoln inquires about me. I assure him all is well, a statement he has reason to doubt. Up again.

Being very careful where I place my right foot, I return to my former high point. The cactus is still there. I ease one hand at a time around and above eager spines. I grip both sides of the gritty crack and apply counterpressure. I arch my body, ease my feet up and out.

At last I attain the ideal position for cactus passing. My legs are curved outwards like those of a rode cowboy who has just mounted a bull. Cowboys, though, usually don't sit on the bull's horns. I glance down between my legs. Thorns, not horns. But big thorns.

This is cause for fear.

This is greater cause for laughter. The giggles are coming. If I surrender, I know I'll pay. Possible future generations of Waltons will pay. Climbing is about self-discipline, no? Don't laugh. Don't laugh.

Don't laugh.

I stop five feet above the cactus. Now, laugh.

Lincoln calls, "What's so funny?"

You'll see, my friend. You'll see. This is one of those

times it's nice to have a partner.

Protection? I lift up one of my embarrassed hexes. I fiddle with it until it rests lightly in the rounded crack. It won't stand a kiss from Snow White, but it's the best I can do.

Runout. Rotten scale. Fifteen feet, twenty. Grit, flakes, gritty-flakes, thirty feet. Even the flared crack is gone now, forty feet. The rock backs off, fifty feet. Gravel, decomposed granite on slabs, sixty feet.

Lincoln calls. End of the rope. Numerous loose monsters are lying about, waiting for a chance to bomb him, take care. Belay? I can just reach a solid manzanita trunk. The gear sling and those two lonely, long-runnered hexes strung together around the tree make a belay. I call down. Lincoln begins to climb.

As he makes the first few moves, I look up and out. The world has changed. A storm, no meek rumbler today, swirls among the peaks of the Sierra Crest. Crags, pines, desert—all so beautiful beneath the sun—are now stark and pure beneath roiling clouds. Dark lines of rain swing like swords above our heads. Fat drops pelt hard but briefly about me.

Ah, Lincoln, that's not what you need.

He's past the crux—quickly—and seems not-at-all fazed by the storm's overpowering presence. Up to the ledge and up the crack he proceeds with alacrity. He reaches the cactus. A pause ensues.

I call down. An indeterminate answer floats up. He scrabbles, comes on the rope. He thrashes and again comes on. I query him again, my eye on blue-black clouds spilling down over Thor.

He says that he's out of gas and can't make it.

Hmmm.

It certainly isn't what I want to hear. Lincoln doesn't complain about pain, fear, or fatigue. He doesn't quit. This has never happened before. No reasonable lines of action come into my mind. I open my mouth and begin to speak some useless words of general encouragement when the storm lends a hand.

ZZZZZZZZZZZZZZZGGGBBBBRRRRAAAAAAAASSSSSH!

Lightening.

Definitely lightning, possibly two hundred yards away and slightly above our belay. Woooo.

I look back down the rope and hope that Lincoln has noticed. He has.

The rope has gone slack. I begin pulling it in quickly. No Lincoln. The old man is gaining altitude fast. I reel in twenty feet before I feel him. I keep on reeling. He isn't slowing down.

See, Lincoln, that bush wasn't so hard, after all. You needed inspiration. You got it.

He arrives at the belay smiling a little sheepishly. Hey, no need for explanations or excuses!

We pack up in record time. No more lightening strikes come close. None need to. The boys can take a hint. We ooze down the third-class chimney and thrash down to the road.

Emerging on the pavement, I glance at my legs—yes, against all experience and better judgment, I have worn shorts to climb in—and find them to be a mass of bloody scratches. No matter. At least I didn't get an electric haircut.

The storm tightens like a black fist above us. Its big punch holds off, though, until we get back to camp. Sitting under huge trees and eating good salami, we watch rain plunge down at last, curtains and extravagant scarves of rain. Pine needles are so thick above us that only a fine mist of drops actually penetrates to us. All is peaceful and safe. I feel like a very small elf hidden beneath a very large mushroom.

The night is dark. Bonzo sleeps near. Bad dreams trouble me. I awake at 3 a.m. thinking that Lincoln is dead. I rise, pretend to get a drink of water, peer over at him. He's snoring loudly. Strange. Where do the fears, the dark visions come from? It's probably best that we don't know.

We roll out before dawn. Packing takes ten minutes with only one inspection of the ground. We bid the Portal farewell and drive up out of the campground to the main road.

Around the first big corner we see the desert. Red-gold, yellow-orange—a complex forest of clouds burns with dawn flames. Red sky in morning. I watch in awe as I slowly follow Lincoln down the big curves. I chuckle nastily as we reach the flatlands. That tent city up in the lap of Whitney won't look much like LA. today.

We drive on down through the Alabama Hills to Lone Pine and the Sportsman's Cafe—black coffee, eggs over easy, home-fries.

Professor of Adventure

by Terry Gifford

Millican Dalton's publicity shot of his belaying technique!
Photo from the Hankinson collection

We are coming to the end of an era in the history of British rockclimbing. First there was the gully era, then that of arêtes, followed by the steep faces, until the era of bold overhanging and sometimes loose rock. Today bolts, climbing walls and competitions are putting an end to the era of risk and adventure in the history of the *development* of the sport. We are in a transitional stage. It seems a good time to look back on the life of a character who epitomizes the spirit of anarchic fun to be had in the outdoors before the sport turned away from nature and became intensely po-faced.

I first met him on Pencoed Pillar, the Hard V Diff that gets you to the narrow summit of the Matterhorn of Mid-Wales. He was chuckling to himself as we sat there looking across the cwm to Cader Idris and Norman was saying, "Brilliant line, crap route!" I glanced behind Norman to the lean grinning figure with the pointed beard and broad-brimmed hat with a pheasant's feather. His obviously homemade clothes were of leather, like his face, and his heavily nailed boots were sockless. He sucked on his Woodbine as if it were oxygen.

"What did you expect?" I whispered to Norman. "You're talking about a route put up by a Professor of Adventure who was noted for fresh air and fun!"

The leather man lit another Woodbine.

"Not that Millican Dalton character!" Norman shouted. "The one dressed like Robinson Crusoe? No wonder this route's more mud than rock! That eccentric guy who lived in a cave in Borrowdale? That's where Sumner should be, for giving this route three stars!"

I glanced over Norman's shoulder, but the Alpine gnome had disappeared. It was to be the first of several uncanny meetings over the following years as each visit to the Lakes included a search for signs of Millican Dalton. In 1903 he'd climbed Pencoed Pillar at the age of thirty-six, just after he'd packed in the London office life and moved in to a hut in Epping Forest, which was to remain his winter home until he died at the age of eighty soon after it burned down. At first he spent his summers in a tent beside Shepherds Crag, then he moved into the cave under Castle Crag, which is still known locally as 'Millican Dalton's Cave.'

My next encounter with his spirit was in the twinkling eyes of Harry Griffin, a man who still refers to the Lake District as "the district."

"Yes, I used to bump into him before the war in Rosthwaite, coming out of Plaskett's with his shopping. He'd hang it from the crossbar of his bike with ropes and bits of camping equipment. He used his bike like a wheelbarrow. He was a genial, kindly man who would be glad to talk about anything. Born in Cumberland, of course, at Alston. Do you know it? No? You don't know the district very well, do you!

"Well, I'd seen his picture in Keswick before I first met him. He had posters in the Abrahams' photographic studio and in Arden's bookshop advertising himself as 'Professor of Adventure' offering 'Camping Holidays, Mountain Rapid Shooting, Rafting, Hair-Breadth Escapes.' He can't have been the first professional guide in the Lakes because there was Gaspard, the Dauphiné guide, at the Wasdale Head before the First World War, but he'd take people up the Needle or into Dove Nest Caves. That was his favourite place. He wrote a guide about it for the *Fell and Rock Journal.*"

Millican Dalton climbed new routes there in 1897 although they're no longer recorded since rockfall has rendered the place unsafe. His friends called this "the rock gym" because they could practice so many different techniques within "150 feet square." Yes, they trained, took their skills seriously in order to do daft things in all weathers on real rock.

"I've written most of what I know of Millican Dalton in *Still the Real Lakeland.* Now you will mention that if you use it, won't you, because I think it's only fair, you know."

It was obvious that in this eighty-year-old teaser the spirit of Millican Dalton was not dead.

Meeting Alan Hankinson, the respected historian of Lake District climbing, soon after this, at the opening of an art exhibition in Cockermouth, was pure luck. I was introduced to "Hank," as he's apparently known locally. At a mention of the name "Millican Dalton," Hank's big white eyebrows suddenly shot up, and he fixed me with a historian's stare.

"Did you know," he said, "that Ken Russell wanted to make a film about him with Spike Milligan in the part?"

We both burst out laughing. Here once again was that warmth generated by Millican Dalton's ghost.

"He's my favorite local character," the white-haired historian confessed. "He was vegetarian, teetotal and a pacifist, and in 1942 he wrote to Churchill from his cave in Castle Rock, asking him to stop the war."

In his writing about Millican, Hankinson emphasizes the balance between a fun-lover living off the land and a serious thinker who carefully considered his own lifestyle. Millican's Quaker education led to an admiration for George Bernard Shaw and then, at the age of about thirty, a life of self-sufficiency exchanging handmade camping equipment for food and adventures for cigarettes. He preferred to avoid money. He slept under an eiderdown and knew where the best hazelnuts grew beside the River Derwent. His clients were instructed in both knots and philosophy. They often came back for more of both. One of them was Mabel Barker, who eventually wrote a memoir in the *Fell and Rock Journal.* Alan Hankinson had hinted that her nephew living in Caldbeck had family photo albums. There Millican Dalton came to life again in amusing family folklore.

Mabel Barker was a teacher who, in 1913, hired tents from the Professor of Adventure for her pupils coming up from Saffron Walden in the Deep South of England for a camping holiday in Borrowdale. Millican offered to take them climbing—and Mabel too. So began the climbing career of the first woman to climb Central Buttress on Scafell. She eventually came to know Millican well during her life running a school in Caldbeck. Now Arnold Barker, her brother's son, was showing me his parents' wedding photograph. It was tiny, the size of the original negative. I had an enlargement made for him and could see Mabel, at the back of Rosthwaite church, rope over her shoulders, standing next to her brother, with rucksack straps pulling back his tweed jacket. His new wife was sneaking a hand into his pocket. Next to her, Millican Dalton, the best man, stood fag in mouth, rope under his leather jacket and full sack on his back, itching to take them all climbing. The night before, Mabel had camped with the bride beside Shepherds Crag, whilst the groom had slept in the cave with the best man. Millican, Mabel wrote, "cooked the wedding breakfast—a chicken boiled in a billy can—in the slate caves, and we spent a happy day climbing in and around the quarries."

"Mabel always used to say," her nephew remembered with a wry smile, "that Millican got dressed up for the wedding. He put socks on! But he sat down on the grass outside the church and took them off again straight afterwards."

The official *Fell and Rock* obituary reveals that Millican "somewhat scandalized his generation by introducing mixed camping tours." In her memoir Mabel Barker wrote about the Professor leading just such a camping trip to the Zillerthal in 1922 when "five of us—four women and Millican—got caught in a blizzard and benighted high up at glacier level above the Alpenrose, and spent a very uncomfortable night out in the snow. A violent thunderstorm added excitement to the situation, the lightening striking on our ice-axes, while drops of water on our hair shone strangely, so that for once at least we wore halos. Perhaps we deserved them, for though drenched to the skin before we gave up the attempt to get down, and all very cold, we sang songs and told stories throughout the long night, and nobody 'woke up dead.'"

Her nephew produced Mabel's photo album of that 1922 Alpine trip. It reveals the sockless Professor, fag in mouth, leading his clients across glaciers like a Pied Piper. They are remarkable period pictures, which have never been published, and they catch the infectious fun that seems to be running along the rope between them.

An unexpected meeting with Millican occurred in Little Langdale Post Office. It is run by Marion, the young daughter of Vince Veevers, best known as the unintentional author of a popular Severe called Ardus on Shepherd's Crag. He'd recorded it as Audus, to preserve the maiden name of his new wife, Elizabeth. "He always did have terrible handwriting," Marion says. "Just before he was killed he'd been talking about reclimbing some of the routes he did with Jim Birkett. He was still very fit." Vince Veevers was killed in 1989 by a runaway lorry that rolled, driverless, down a lane in Shropshire where he lived.

A casual mention of the magic words "Millican Dalton" in Marion's Post Office produced a family story from the late 1920s:

"Dad had cycled to the Lakes from Bolton and was carrying his bike over Styhead to Wasdale when he saw someone climbing on Kern Knotts, so he went over to have a look. A voice called down, 'Can you tie a bowline?' Dad shouted up "Yes!' Actually he couldn't. He had to ask a passing climber to show him. That was his first climb, Kern Knotts Chimney, and when he got to the top of it, he met Millican Dalton holding the rope. In fact, he didn't get a chance to climb again for some time, but he was sure that he definitely wanted to take it up after that first introduction."

In 1940, seven years before Millican died, Vince Veevers was back on Gable with Jim Birkett climbing the impressive line of Tophet Grooves (HVS 5b). Millican's kindly offer to the stranger seemed to be not only typical of his own enjoyment in giving adventures to just anyone but also of the way the torch was passed on in his era.

But where was Millican's cave? "We could tell he was 'at home,'" Mabel wrote, "by the blue smoke curling among the trees, easily seen from the Borrowdale road." I searched downwards from the top of Castle Crag until, almost at the path, on the northeast corner, I found some quarries. I noted an amazingly colourful 'painted' wall to tip off Gordon Stainforth for his Lakeland book, wandered up to a big cave and hit a roadway leading up to another, in the high corner of which was a hole. This appeared to be "The Attic," the Professor's cave. Confirmation came as I passed a wall to the outside. Unforgivably cut into the rock is Millican's now historical enigmatic message: "Don't!! Waste Words, Jump to Conclusions".

From here the Professor took clients sailing on Derwentwater under his famous red sails, rafting down the rapids of Borrowdale on "Rogue Herries" made from rubbish scavenged at Grange tip, climbing and caving by candlelight in Dove Nest, tree climbing, which he called "Tree Boling," gill scrambling up Lodore Falls in spate and camping with instruction on the best woods for fire-lighting, all laced with a philosophy that was actually being lived out.

It's ironical that some of the people today who take government money to introduce the young to adventure in the Lake District are the very people who are taking the rock itself, our rock, into this new bolted era. It is sickening to find bolt holes at the top of the bouldering slabs at Seathwaite, in Borrowdale, for example. You won't meet the spirit of Millican Dalton there any longer. Nor at the top of Farm Buttress in the quiet valley of Martindale. Those who left three abseil chains and six bolts there probably thought they could defile our rock and get away with it. What adventure in raw nature they've left for you when you get around to exploring these untouched secluded areas! And you won't meet Millican's spirit of adventure any longer in his own larger cave where the litter from overnighters makes it just like any other urban quarry.

But you can meet him in other people and other places in the Lake District still, I hope. And before it's too late, we must raise a voice against the defilement of *all* of our vertical fields of adventure.

The 28-Year Itch

by Allison Carpenter

Author at summit of "Zodiac" Photo by Gary Carpenter-Koch

When I picked up the photos of our October ascent of "Zodiac" on El Capitan, I envisioned myself lanky and blond, flashing a grin at the camera, sort of a Daryl Hannah in étriers. The bulging envelope of photos testified otherwise. What I saw resembled the poster child for a Leprosy Climb-a-thon. Close inspection revealed arms riddled with angry scabs, a shirt encrusted with ghastly stains reminiscent of erupted blisters, thighs crawling with weeping sores. A little makeup, and I could pass as "The Fly." All this from a little brush with poison oak.

Gary, my old climbing partner and new boyfriend, declared my affliction the most disgusting case of poison oak he'd ever seen. Fortunately we were still in the honeymoon state, so I took it as a compliment. Unbearable, however, was itchiness that began shortly before we planned to start up El Cap. I lay awake nights, anxiously trying not to scratch at the welts that crept over my body.

Frankly, Gary and I, fledgling big wall climbers both, entertained doubts about climbing Zodiac. It is notoriously steep. But this route has become something of a mecca for aid climbers ever since it was put up by Charlie Porter climbing solo in 1972. At that time, Zodiac was rated A4 and A5 but has been downrated to A3. This is a level of difficulty tailor-made for the aid climber who is smart enough to use pitons, hooks, rivet hangers, and a portaledge—and dumb enough to want to.

Some of our doubts were appeased by a stranger who appeared in El Cap Meadows the day before we began our ascent. The blond, fortyish man, who resembled a Campbell's Soup Kid, asked us which route we were climbing, as we racked up over icy slurps of our ubiquitous Kamikazes.

"The Zodiac," we slurred.

"Oh really," commented the Campbell's Soup Kid. "Great. That's a route I put up back in 1972."

Gary and I smirked and thought, yeah, right, and you're Charlie Porter, too.

"What's your name?" I asked, feeling quite clever to have trapped him.

"Charlie Porter," replied the Soup Kid. Being a cool big wall climber, I gasped and practically stumbled onto him. "Really?" I gushed. "Tell us about the Zodiac."

Porter was friendly and generous with information, which cast further doubt on his authenticity as a big wall climber. But he was the real Charlie Porter, and lived with his Chilean wife on the island of Chiloe, Chile. As if a colorful and prolific climbing career weren't enough, Porter now conducts geo-archaeological research expeditions to Patagonia and the Antarctic.

His stories of climbing El Cap were modestly told but revealed that our Soup Kid was no Stay-Puff. On one solo first ascent, Porter accidently dropped his sleeping gear and proceeded to finish the climb. He slept in slings with a foam pad clenched around him. We sheepishly looked at Gary's double-wide portaledge. We then eyed the stacks of high-tech camming devices that surplant piton placements over much of Zodiac. I felt our ascent pale next to Porter's pioneering efforts, which included many routes on El Cap, and the first solo of the Cassin Ridge on Denali in 1977. But the purpose of our ascent of El Cap was not to open up new terrain. It was to explore the realm of our individual strengths and capabilities. Porter supported our quest with encouraging tidbits.

"The great thing about the Zodiac," he told us, "is that it's nice and clean."

"Really?" I said, thinking that he was comparing it cleanliness to the infamous poop-strewn ledges of the Nose.

"Yes," continued Porter brightly, "It's so steep that if you screw up, you get a nice, clean fall."

I whimpered. I really have no internal compulsion to climb steep aid routes. But it is an ugly truth that I seek a tiny measure of immortality through climbing. Deep down, every time I plunk down my credit card at the climbing store, I want the clerk to freeze, look up, and say, "Not *the* Allison Carpenter? The one who climbed 'Zodiac' in a remarkable five-day push?"

So the next morning, propelled by vanity, I was leading out through a roof on the second pitch. I was bawling like a baby.

"I'm scared!" I sobbed shamelessly as I dangled 100 feet from the ground. You would think I'd never aid climbed before. I wished I'd never started.

"Just test each piece," advised Gary. "Jump on your aiders, then step up and don't think about that piece any more."

I gingerly eased onto my pro, a No.2 Friend that would

have held a Volkswagen.

"Jump!" commanded Gary.

Still gripping my last piece I gave a dainty bounce. Gary rolled his eyes. He said nothing but I recognized the look. "Sissy!" it said. I glowered, launched onto the étrier and jumped feverishly. The Friend didn't budge. I continued up, testing my pro, becoming more confident with each overhanging placement.

Gary is an excellent belayer to have on a big wall. As soon as I am a few feet from the belay, he busies himself arranging gear, eating, taking photos, and daydreaming, rarely concerning himself with the drama unfolding at my end of the rope. By the time he finishes cleaning my pitch, he has cheerfully forgotten about my incoherent babbling and wails of anxiety, in addition to other more pungent remarks about aid climbing.

As Gary began the next pitch, I contemplated my precarious position. I'd come a long way from learning to climb with my dad in the North Cascades. In college, I had climbed Half Dome with Gary and Rolf, an erstwhile climbing partner of mine and a charter member of the Tippy Turtle Alpine Groupe. This was an exclusive cadre of young climbers who had found their calling in drinking, and later puking, in the parking lot at Index Town Wall. At that time, neither Rolf nor I had made up our minds about Gary, a farmer/philosopher from Willamette Valley. Gary tended to prefer Grape Nuts and yoghurt to the donuts Rolf and I scavenged from abandoned trays at the Yosemite Lodge cafeteria. On the other hand, he could drink lots of cheap beer while ranting and raving about the ills of society. Rolf and I worked hard to represent the ills of society, so we were quietly pleased with Gary's tirades. Even negative attention was better than none.

Now, however, I was 28. I'd long been excommunicated from the Tippy Turtles, including Rolf. I'd recently broken up with a guy who had strained all the self-esteem I'd ever possessed. (There wasn't much anyway, ever since about the first day of school in seventh grade.) I was even developing a taste for Grape Nuts. It seemed natural that Gary and I had suddenly fallen in love and bought a house together. All of this pointed toward a need for security, solid ground. Instead, I was perched at a hanging belay on El Cap feeling the rope inch out between my fingers.

"Watch me!" I heard Gary yell from above.

"I'm watching!" I cried, as I stared emptily into space.

I studied my cuticles, already beginning to crack and become grouted with sweat, dirt, and aluminum dust. Far below, a cattle trailer full of tourists pulled over, and a muffled, rehearsed speech droned from a bullhorn. "Blah, blah, blah, El Capitan, blah, blah, men climbing up ropes, blah, blah, blah..."

I began crooning my limited and off-key repertoire of songs with a tune by Traffic and degenerated from there. I wound up my set with a few Syd Barrett lyrics. Only then did I lapse into the unavoidable boredom engendered by big wall belays.

Gary finished his pitch late in the day. Enough time to haul, jug, clean, and gulp down some Spaghettios. Now came the moment I dreaded: bedtime. As soon as I stopped moving, the poison oak kicked in. I scratched my armpits, my ankles, my back. I panted. I tried to count to 30 without scratching but made it to twelve, only to violently scratch myself all over.

The next four nights resembled a professional wrestling match: my opponent, an invisible, systemic poison far more insidious than some undressed, overpaid bodybuilder. Exhausted from climbing and worried by our ever-tightening water rations, I writhed on the portaledge scratching my wounds as the full moon bathed us in unbearable light. Even Gary could not sleep under its interrogating glare.

For our nightly entertainment, a party of Spaniards struggled up Zenyatta Mondatta to our left. They climbed around the clock. At dark, we would watch the headlamps of the night shift come on as the Spaniards nailed until 3 a.m., even 5 a.m. Gary and I tried to think up a Zen koan for it: *One person, tormented with insane itching, lies on a tiny platform. Another pounds pitons all nights. Who is the greater fool?* As with all Zen koans, the answer remained enigmatic.

As we progressed up Zodiac, Gary and I found our new intimacy threatening at first. We'd never climbed together since falling in love, and I worried that our climbing partnership would be jeopardized by this intense development. But some aspects of climbing a wall were easier with a partner with whom one was intimate: going to the bathroom, for example. This involved Gary counterbalancing the portaledge on one end while I shat into a paper bag at the other. Because our environmental awareness was not expanded enough to haul these bags to the top, we flung them to the bottom, which was great fun.

My chief fear in climbing with Gary, however, lay not in our intimacy, but in an inferiority complex I'd had ever since we met eight years ago: to wit, my lesser climbing ability. We had staggered the leads so that although we swapped pitches, he would lead the crux pitches. At times I felt like a belay Bunny.

"You're doing your share," insisted Gary. "But hey, if you really feel bad, you can have one of my leads."

"Ha, ha, ha!" I said cheerfully. "Just kidding. I love A2. Really."

Secretly, I found even the easier leads intimidating. Although fixed pro adorned the route, it often involved copperheads with manky webbing and rusty bolt nubbins without nuts or hangers. I operated on the principle that whoever used the piece last outweighed my 130 pounds—not a principle that would save me in a fall but an adequate psychological crutch for my fear-crippled brain.

The third day found me needing more than a psychological crutch, however. I needed some sort of wheelchair. I had started up an overhanging bolt ladder, which led to a roof that was supposedly A1, and I was shaking like I had DT's. Gary couldn't decide if he should talk me through it or offer me a cigarette. I don't smoke.

"It shouldn't be too hard," he coaxed. "Just top-step your aiders, and you should be able to get a good pin under the roof. You can do it."

Tears of frustration and embarrassment washed down my grimy face.

"He doesn't mean it," I thought. "He's thinking, 'Why don't I have a girlfriend who hikes to the summit of El Cap with beer for me when I top out?"

I managed to high-step, only to confront a shallow pod under the roof, into which I nested an angle and a leeper. Ignoring Gary's calm rational voice, I stared at the pitons, paralyzed. The gears in my head whirred, but my body remained frozen. I stared out at the valley, listened to the wind, then watched a jet streak overhead. I pictured myself a passenger on the jet, whisked along by some faceless pilot as I ate peanuts and skimmed a meaningless in-flight magazine.

Gradually, my mind turned blank. I began mechanically testing the pitons, then stepping up, adjusting my body to the tight accommodations of a low roof, One stacked piton placement followed another. I crammed a TCU in once, but it failed, and dropped me with a thud onto a tied-off pin. I moved in a tiny sphere of awareness as I inched toward the outer edge of the roof, miles away. Somewhere along the space-time continuum, the seam grew, first a thin gap against the wall, now a bona fide crack that accepted #3 and #4 friends.

"How's it going?" called Gary. "Are you getting some

good pro now?"

I didn't answer, afraid that by admitting that I was safe, I would break the spell that propelled me upward. Easy aid soon led me to the belay, however. I tied off, pulled Betty (our haulbag), and basked in the sun until Gary jugged up.

"Guess what you just did," he said.

"Set an endurance record for the longest time spent on an A1 pitch," I muttered.

"Nope. You just climbed an A3 pitch," he grinned. Your copy of the topo was wrong. It left out the A3 nailing under the roof."

"Wow!" I whooped. "A3, huh? Piece of cake! Hey aren't you glad I'm climbing with you instead of hiking to the top to bring you beer?"

Gary thought for a moment. I kicked him.

"Yeah!" he piped.

After this, there was more hard climbing, but we had each done our crux pitches. Our severe water shortage was alleviated on the fourth day when we reached a ledge upon which someone had left two gallons of water. This water cache transformed the rest of the route. What had been a hike in the desert with the French foreign legion became a frolic in the park. The final pitch overhung at the top and required a desperate, undignified wallow to the summit block.

A few days later, in search of the politically correct solution to the consequences of flinging our potty bags to the talus below El Cap, I hiked to the base of the route with a huge garbage bag—and latex gloves. Behind my hazardous waste cleanup mission lay hopes of finding a Friend that I had dropped. I didn't find the Friend, but I recovered a lot of stinky bags that proclaimed, "Keep Yosemite Clean—Return Bag for 5 Cent Refund."

With my obligation to society fulfilled, the following day

we cruised out of the valley and stopped on our way at the Wawona Inn for Sunday brunch. I was coated with every topical anti-itch ointment available, and my slimy white skin drew glances from well-heeled tourists in tennis sweaters. I didn't care. We gorged on Belgian waffles, omelettes, biscuits and gravy, fruit, danishes. I finally pushed away my third plate of blueberry cheesecake with whipped cream and left the last bite untouched as a monument to my self-will. Gary finished his hash browns and leaned back cautiously in his chair after rapidly shifting his center of balance with several pounds of food.

"What are you thinking about?" he asked.

"My Saturn return," I replied.

"Your what?" he asked.

"My Saturn return," I explained. "That's what happens to women around the age of 28. Saturn returns to the position it held at your birth. If you don't accept new responsibilities and commitments, it can totally screw you up."

"I didn't know Saturn was ever around in the first place," said Gary.

"Well, I didn't either, until some of my weirder friends told me about it," I admitted. "The good news is, you can head off Saturn by drastically altering the course of your life in some positive, enriching way."

"Such as contracting poison oak, then climbing a big wall?" Gary said sardonically.

"Yeah," I concluded. "Love, poison oak, and big walls as a rite of passage! What do you think?"

Gary gazed at me thoughtfully, "I think you've been in the sun too long."

I nodded in agreement, smiled, and began to scratch a new itch.

The Great 1941 Devil's Tower Rescue

by Richard Bennett

Early on the morning of October 1, 1941, Newell Joyner, Custodian of Devil's Tower National Monument, discussed with a clerk in his office a rumor of a parachute Jump onto Devil's Tower. The two had noted some increase in airplane activity over the Monument in recent days but were not unduly concerned. After all, for two dollars one could take an aerial tour over the Tower and Little Missouri Buttes. The views were spectacular. Besides, who would be crazy enough to consider such an action? For as Joyner remembered asking, "How could they get down?"

Looking something like a gigantic inverted and truncated ice cream cone, Devil's Tower rises precipitously and incongruously above the rolling landscape of northeastern Wyoming. Although climbers have been aware of the rock for more than half a century, most people are familiar with it from the film *Close encounters of the Third Kind,* in which actor Richard Dreyfus scrambles up—so Hollywood makes it appear—to meet a bunch of amiable aliens. In reality, except for the occasional iron-nerved soloist, all ascents of the rock are technical climbs.

In 1941 the Tower's walls had been climbed only a few times—the routes were considered among the most severe accomplished in the country. Two local ranchers had in fact climbed the rock by pounding in a line of wooden pegs on the Fourth of July in 1893, but the Tower was not free climbed until Fritz Wiessner's ascent in 1937.

In his time George Hopkins was probably the best parachutist in the world. He held various records including the greatest number of jumps, the longest delayed jump, and the highest jump in the United States. A 30-year-old Texan, Hopkins was more than just a daredevil: sympathetic to the plight of England, in 1939 he had instructed in the Royal Air Force and also earned distinction as a transport pilot in the evacuation of British soldiers from Dunkirk.

At 8:15 a.m. on October 1, right about the moment Custodian Joyner was pronouncing that nobody was foolish enough to do it, George Hopkins jumped from an airplane above the Tower. In one of his many notes thrown down after his successful landing, Hopkins wrote, "It was to let people know just what a person can do with a parachute if they really know their parachutes. I had also wanted to get a 'chute so I could prove that I could hit the impossible, and this is it and I could do it again." Besides, Hopkins had a fifty dollar bet with Earl Brockelsby of Rapid City, South Dakota that he could do it.

But more germane was that two weeks later in Rapid City, Hopkins was to attempt to break the world record for the most parachute jumps done in one day. Hopkins had the backing of the Rapid City Junior Chamber of Commerce for the exploit, and the Tower escapade was publicity for the forthcoming event.

How to get down from Devil's Tower? *No problem.* The plane's pilot made another pass and dropped a 1000-foot, ½-inch Manila rope. Unfortunately, it missed. And therein begins a six-day tale that soon held the attention of the entire nation.

Joyner, hiking up to the base of the mountain, encountered Earl Brockelsby, and learned who was on Devil's Tower. The Custodian was not amused and ordered Hopkins' backers to get the parachutist off the Tower. After considerable delay, another pilot, Clyde Ice of Spearfish, South Dakota dropped a second rope and a grappling hook, but Hopkins soon reported the rope was hopelessly tangled. The weather showed signs of changing, and the wind was increasing. At dusk a drop of blankets and food was made, and Hopkins retired for the night.

Hopkins did not reappear until 9 a.m. the following morning. He then dropped a note (tied to a rock) stating he was OK but his arms felt weak. Some rain had fallen, temperatures were near freezing, and the wind was blowing hard. Joyner, Ice and Brockelsby assembled at the base of the Tower. Several reporters were present as well. In his report to the National Park Service on the episode, Joyner wrote, "Many schemes were being proposed; no one seemed to have the position of director; no one seemed to be in a position to judge the practicability of the various schemes proposed."

Hopkins' own plan—he was ignorant of the technique of rappeling— was to descend the near-vertical upper 650 feet of the Tower hand over hand down the rope, which he had by then untangled. Whether this feat was even possible soon became academic, because the rope Hopkins threw down snagged some 200 feet from the top.

Helicopters were new to the world, but such rescue was discussed. In Joyner's report he noted that a "helicopter can descend or ascend vertically or else hover at any designated point a few feet off the ground." Air currents around the mountain, however, were known to be unpredictable and dangerous, and it was decided to contact a helicopter manufacturing company for more information.

But Newell Joyner had seen the Tower climbed, and he strongly advocated that experienced climbers scale the mountain to assist Hopkins down. The Rapid City group finally agreed, and they asked Joyner to take charge of the rescue. In the mean time, pilot Ice dropped more food, clothing, a tent, a healthy supply of whiskey, and, perhaps for good measure, yet another 1000-foot rope—the third. Alas, it bounced and rolled off the northwest side of the Tower.

Prior to late afternoon of this the second day, the reporters felt they were covering a publicity stunt, but now they saw real *news* and jostled to use the one telephone line serving the Monument. Soon telegraph wires were humming and the airwaves were crackling. Devil's Tower National Monument needed climbers to rescue a man marooned on its top. And not just a man, but a man who had already volunteered his services against the rising tide of the Axis powers. The news was like an electric charge across the nation.

To appreciate the media coverage, one needs to understand America in 1941. The nation was racked with indecision about whether to go to war. With growing anxiety America had watched Hitler's *blitzkrieg* ravage Europe. Country after country had fallen before the Nazi terror. American ships had been fired upon in the North Atlantic. In Asia, Japan fought its bloody war in China, and in July of 1941 invaded Indonesia.

In the midst of this quagmire of gloom and uncertainty came the ridiculous story of a patriotic parachutist stuck on a big rock in Wyoming. Perhaps a kind of mass psychic release occurred, because for a few days at least, the nation watched with increasing interest the plight of one George Hopkins.

On the evening of October 2, Joyner received a telegram which read, "Unique first descent need any help completing it?" The telegram was from Jack Durrance. Durrance had established an impressive record of first ascents in the Tetons (including the Exum Direct, the North Face, and West Face of the Grand) and had been on Fritz Wiessner's ill-fated and controversial 1939 attempt on K2. He was also one of the few climbers who had ever summited Devil's Tower. But Durrance was not alone in responding to the call. Some of the country's best mountaineers were tossing gear in their trunks and heading for Wyoming.

But the first plan was to accomplish the rescue with climbers from within the Park Service. The next morning Ernest Field, a ranger from Rocky Mountain National Park, and Warren Gorrell, a guide there, arrived at Devil's Tower after driving most of the night through bad weather. Field had previously studied the climbing routes established on the mountain, and the two men decided to try the route put up by Jack Durrance and Harrison Butterworth in 1938.

After some easy terrain was crossed, the men reached a leaning, slightly detached column which they negotiated with difficulty. At the top of the column was a fearsome section of rock. Field wrote, "We looked at it, and then at each other, and then back up the pitch again." Two parallel cracks, about a foot and a half apart, ran up the dead-vertical section of rock for about 80 feet. (This pitch, the crux of the Durrance route, is now rated a 5.7.) Try as they might, the men could make no further progress. In one attempt Field took a ten-foot fall and bruised his side. They decided to descend.

During the day spectators and more reporters assembled around the Monument. One reporter wrote there had not been this much excitement in the area since the cricket infestations of the late-'30s. State highway patrolmen and boy scouts volunteered to help manage the parking and the swelling crowds.

As dusk came it was clear Hopkins was in for another night. Field and Gorrell strongly recommended that Durrance's offer be accepted, and he was called at his home in Hanover, New Hampshire. The young climber immediately left for New York City to catch a morning flight to Cheyenne.

On Saturday, October 4, the crowds poured into the Monument. Now concerns with injury on the ground became nearly as pressing as Hopkins' situation above. A plea was made to other National Parks for more personnel to help handle the throngs. The weather was bad, and to the utter frustration of the press, the one phone line occasionally went dead.

That afternoon Durrance's plane was grounded in Chicago due to the poor weather, and he boarded a train bound for Denver to fly from there. At about the same time, the Goodyear Company of Akron, Ohio, called and offered the services of the Goodyear Blimp. Although the blimp could not arrive for several days, the offer was accepted. Joyner worried that the weather might continue to be poor and that a climb would not be feasible. The press greeted the information on the blimp with great enthusiasm. A new dimension of interest had been added: Now **the race** was on to rescue Hopkins. The headlines grew larger daily.

The only one unriled by all the commotion was George Hopkins himself. Hopkins was, seemingly at least, having a rather good time of it. After all, he now had a tent and enough supplies to outfit a small army. His notes took on a cavalier tone. In one he wrote, "If you get a chance, send up my morning paper." Hopkins began to sign his notes as "Devil's Tower George."

Monument officials learned that another climber would be arriving. Paul Petzoldt, a Teton climbing guide, was also one of America's premier climbers. Besides having accomplished numerous first ascents in the Tetons, Petzoldt had been on the first American expedition to K2 in 1938. Unfortunately, Petzoldt and Durrance had been competitive in the Tetons, and there was no love lost between the two men.

October 5 broke wet and cold. Even the usually cheerful Hopkins sent down a note complaining of the weather. But he also asked that a "brunette or even a red head" be dropped down, since his previous request for a "blond" had been denied. On the ground the dreary weather did not deter spectators, and the crowds continued to pour in.

Newspaper accounts estimate between 3,000 and 4,000 people had assembled. Many had set up tents and were camping for the whole show.

The weather was causing continuing problems with Jack Durrance. During the day his plane, enroute from Denver to Cheyenne, had turned around because of the poor conditions. Maybe, the press speculated, like the tortoise and the hare, the blimp would win the race.

As cold October 5 passed into evening, word came that Durrance had rendez-voused with three other climbers, and they were driving at full speed with highway patrol escort from Denver. With snow falling as Hopkins settled in for his fifth night alone, he surely wondered whether the next day would see him to the ground. No doubt he would have been pleased to see the climbers' cars pull into the monument's parking area at 11:45 p.m..

On October 6 the party of eight climbers (!) set out at first light. The rock was iced up, and it began to snow again, but no one wanted to turn back. Turn back with 4,000 people watching?! At the vertical cracks which had stalled Field and Gorrell, even the veteran Durrance had a hard time of it. Although he had free climbed the section on his ascent of 1938, now conditions were too severe. The men resorted to pounding in wedges of wood for aid.

Petzoldt and Durrance wrangled over how matters should proceed, with one or the other always leading the climb. Petzoldt had an agreement with the press to take photos, and received criticism from Durrance that he was more interested in photography than safety. At some point during the procedure Petzoldt's camera suffered an untimely and unexplained accident. One might speculate that Durrance's dismay at being photographed standing on wooden pegs was connected with this event.

At 3:15 p.m. Durrance and Petzoldt stood on the summit and shook hands with Hopkins. Henry Coulter (who had pioneered climbs in the Tetons), Chappel Cranmer (who with Wiessner had made a serious attempt on Canada's Snowpatch Spire and was on the 1939 K2 team), Merrill McLane, Field and Gorrell, and Harold "Altitude" Rapp (he was 6'10") soon followed. The men found Hopkins in good spirits. He was given a quick demonstration in rappeling, which he mastered readily, and with the sun sinking in the sky, the group started down.

As darkness fell the scene took on a surrealistic aura. From high on the walls of the Tower could be heard the calls and yodels of the descending climbers. On the ground thousands warmed themselves around innumerable fires and watched and waited. Sometimes spectators would yodel in encouragement to those above, or shout out some inane instruction. A huge spotlight was trained on the cliff and the men could be seen moving in and out of the darkness. At 8:20 p.m. they were down. As the throng surged upward, hooting and applauding, Hopkins was heard to say, "I'd rather climb back up the cliff than face that crowd!"

The episode was over. Newspapers from coast to coast gave the rescue a final splash across headlines, then returned to less-appealing yet more-pressing matters. But the people of northeastern Wyoming had enjoyed the best show in half a century. The flamboyant Hopkins received nationwide publicity. Eight climbers made the second ascent of a great climbing route, and for a few days at least, America forgot her troubles.

Where Land is Mostly Sky

by Richard F. Fleck

How clean it was that morning when the three of us unloaded our gear from the car to climb two 14,000-foot peaks in central Colorado near Loveland Pass. It had been reported that the summit of Grays Peak experienced a short but furious downpour of popcorn snow the day before. We all felt a little apprehensive about climbing two peaks on the same day. I hadn't climbed a "fourteener" since my thirty-fifth birthday almost twenty years earlier.

Now I was living in Denver as were my two new companions. Though we were all in our fifties, we remained, nonetheless, eager to climb two peaks in the high tundra where land is mostly sky. The jagged glacial ridge leading up to Grays and Torreys peaks jumped out at us in the clear air. It had an extraterrestrial look—all rock with just the slightest suggestion of green vegetation gleaming in the rising sun.

Down along our trail grew dense groves of willows whose yellowing leaves gently rustled in the morning breeze. Ravens circled high above following the contour of the surrounding glacial cirques. Father George Schroeder led and Mark Reames and I Followed sometimes stopping to admire Colorado columbines and sometimes craning our heads back to look at billowing clouds.

George disappeared around the bend. By the time we reached him, he was on his knees in the subalpine grasses not praying but photographing a whole field of sun-glinted flowers including yellow and rosy paintbrushes, bright-blue hare bells, purple penstemon, and white bistort. "Vincent Van Gogh would have gone wild here." I remarked, and George just grinned.

By now subalpine willows were reduced to mere mats huddled down low and as much as possible out of the wind. We notice some white dots above. Were they mountain goats or just rocks? At last they moved. We continued trudging along the trail and stopped frequently to catch our breath as we were now well above 12,000 feet. People above us stood still looking intently at something. Huffing and puffing, we arrived at their level on the mountain to see a female mountain goat in a shaggy coat with her three kid goats all staring directly at us. Jagged peaks had come into view to the north and east with several other fourteeners including Mount Bierstadt and Mount Evans east of us and Longs Peak to the far north. We could also make out several high thirteeners like Arapaho Peak and Square Top. One year earlier Mark Reames and I sauntered up 13,400-foot Arapaho Peak with its jagged summit looming over Arapaho Glacier, the city of Boulder's water source. Mark recalled that this glacier had receded considerably since the early 1940s. Soon we could not see anything to the south and west save the high, looming slopes of Grays above and Torreys to our right. We had to climb still higher to cast an eye on the Collegiate Range.

The soil we stood on was sparse and rocky. A few tufts of alpine forget-me-nots dotted the landscape of the immediate foreground. From such a perch it is easy to agree with John Muir that the mountaineer climbs mountains with more than his feet and hands: "In like manner the soul sets forth at times upon rambles of its own. Our bodies, though meanwhile out of sight and forgotten, blend into the rest of nature, blind to the boundaries of individuals. But it is after both the body and soul of a mountaineer have worked hard, engaged hard, that they are most palpably separate. Our weary limbs, lying at rest on the pine needles, make no attempt to follow after or sympathize with the nimble spirit, that apparently glad of the opportunity, wanders along down gorges, along beetling cliffs, or away among the peaks and glaciers of the farthest landscapes, or into realms the eye had not seen, nor ear heard; when at length we are ready to return home to our flesh-bone tabernacle, we scarcely for a moment or two know in what direction to seek for it." But our bodies reminded us that they were thirsty and hungry.

The summit look insurmountable. It rose higher and higher. We now stood above 13,000 feet and had become chilly, but not so chilly to make us put on jackets. In the bracing air we slowly edged a bit higher to walk out onto a promontory ridge where we all caught whiffs of fresh forest air from the lower depths. Longs Peak looked close enough to hit with a stone.

More mountain goats appeared on rocky ledges below us. Their beards fluttered in the breeze. Alpine sunflowers, looking like miniature fiery suns, bobbed on their stalks, and tailless pikas let out high-pitched squeaks punctuating our alpine flow of thoughts.

I could make out tiny human figures apparently standing on the top of Grays Peak, which reminded me of my ascent of Mount Fuji where droves of Japanese pilgrims hung over the edge of the volcanic peak to shout words of encouragement to climbers lower down. No tea house here to refresh us, though! Seeing a marmot scurry along the trail encouraged us to keep up our pace, slow though it was. We got to the point where there was nothing but sky all around the rocky ridge just ahead. That ridge eventually yielded until we stood atop it in a little circle of rocks surrounded by a universe of space.

The Mount of the Holy Cross rose to the far southwest, as well as scores of other peaks of the Collegiate Range. And to the extreme southwest we just barely saw the distant Maroon Bells and Snowmass. Like Buddhist monks high in the Himalaya, we turned slowly in circles taking in the cosmos until a sudden shower dumped pellets of popcorn snow in our hair and on our clothing. We smiled.

Out came our sandwiches and juice. We are heartily amid

an August snowstorm at 14,270 feet atop Colorado's ninth highest peak. During our lunch several shaggy mountain goats outstared us with their shiny dark eyes. Far below we could discern a little piece of I-70 with a mad scramble of ant-sized cars heading for the Eisenhower Tunnel. Though we could not see the entrance to the tunnel, we could see the buzzing ants' destination—the wide valley containing Lake Dillon and several ski areas and a dark puff of cloud, which would probably surprise the ants.

George, Mark and I were game to go ahead with our plan to do a second fourteener looming a half mile west of us. We would have to descent a thousand feet or so to the saddle and then painfully regain the altitude lost. Torreys Peak is only three feet lower than Grays. Of course the scramble down to the saddle was a cinch, except for a few wobbly rocks. The sun came out again in full force—a welcome sight, as we passed by several crusty snowfields at the saddle and slightly above. And then as the pitch up steep Torreys increased, I felt my muscles tire, so much so that my two companions slowly distanced themselves from me. All I could see was rock and sky and two guys getting smaller as they edged toward the summit. Every time they paused to photograph a snowfield or a cluster of yellow lichen coating some boulder, I regained ten feet but could never quite catch up. Breathing became difficult. Perhaps the combination of Grays and Torreys was like a right and left hook in the boxing ring. I could no longer see my companions. Was I going to make it?

It suddenly dawned on me that the reason I could not see Mark and George was that they stood on the summit just overhead. They weren't miles away after all. A few huffs and puffs and I saw their faces. A few more, and I saw their entire bodies against the sky. They stood among a herd of mountain goats and George was talking to them.

"Thank you gentlemen for sharing your marvelous home

with us!"

After resting five minutes at 14,267 feet and drinking some cold water, we all felt restored and energetic. Several other climbers joined us and engaged us in a discussion about which mountain range was which and which ski area was Breckenridge as opposed to Keystone. Mark, the native Coloradan, settled these issues with a tone of finality. Before making our descent, we cast one more glance around the universe of alpine terrain of lower reddish ridges, distant gray peaks, azure-blue skies with cumulus clouds, and the distance mass of Mount Evans and Mount Bierstadt to the east perhaps 25 miles away. We tentatively agreed upon climbing one more fourteener, probably Mount Bierstadt, after a two-week sojourn in the city of Denver far below. We waved goodbye to our fellow mountaineers (both humans and goats) and began our rapid descent to the saddle between the peaks.

Halfway down to the saddle, it began to snow again. The sky had become completely gray and the wind increased. Instead of going all the way around the base of Grays graying summit, we looked for cut off trails down the hollow bowl between the peaks. I followed the crest of a snowfield while my two companions took a surer route along the edge of the snow. I told them I would meet them down yonder where the snowfield trail and the talus trail joined perhaps eight hundred vertical feet below.

Just a month earlier I had climbed Saint Mary's Glacier above Idaho Springs to the green tundra to stand and stare at a grazing cow elk some 50 yards distant. When it came time to descend the glacier with its steep pitch, I instinctively traversed from one side to the other instead of going straight down and risking a slip. Today I felt quite comfortable on this snowfield even though it had a rather steep drop-off to jagged rocks 80 feet lower. Apparently this dizzy angle had frightened away Mark and George.

As I traversed the steep snow patch angling down toward the naked rocks, I noticed George and Mark had only begun their descent into the bowl. Nonetheless all three of us edged closer to the rendezvous point in a mixture of pelting sleet and snow. It had become quite nasty, and I was glad to be down in the glacial bowl out of the wind. We were all close enough to talk to each other with our voices echoing off cliffs of talus.

"How's your trail?" I shouted.

"Slick as grease," they shouted back.

Before long we no longer needed to shout. My trail descended rapidly over muddy rills and wobbly rocks. Quite a barren place, I thought to myself as I hadn't noticed so much as one flower.

It was good to rejoin my companions. Grays and Torreys looked like monstrous giants high above. Eventually, there was more grass than rock and happily our trail joined the main trail off Grays Peak. The sun returned full strength, and we stopped to take off our hooded parkas and gulp down some ice-cold water from our canteens.

Since we had expended much energy, the relatively simple descent proved wearisome. George stopped suddenly. We caught up with him and knew why. We listened in silence to the wind in the willows. The sound varied in intensity and pitch with each new gust of wind. Ravens sailed above following the wind currents. Willows, wind and birds soothed our minds and made us forget the pain of our tired feet. We became three winged Mercuries descending the last slope with a message of the mountain's glad tidings.

Mount Bierstadt, rising just west of Mount Evans, was named after the German-born artist Albert Bierstadt (1830-1902). One of the last artists of the Hudson River School of painting, his works being vast panoramas of the

Rocky Mountain West. I remember standing in front of one of his Wagnerian scenes at the Buffalo Bill Center in Cody, Wyoming. A horrendous lightning storm arched itself between two gigantic peaks of the Wind River Mountains of Wyoming. I felt that I could hear the wind, taste the rain, and feel the crackle of electricity (à la Wagner's operas). Though the vegetation was wrong, and the mountains absurdly high, the mood and atmosphere were right. The painting brought me back to the alpine heights of southern Wyoming.

Twelve days after our climb of Grays and Torreys, George Schroeder, I and two new climbing companions, Willy Sutton and Ide Rodman, met at the little town of Grant Colorado at 8 a.m. to drive on Guanella Pass and climb Mount Bierstadt (14,036 feet). The mountain would live up to its namesake by providing us with a Wagnerian overture.

At Guanella Pass we were not certain which trail would lead us to Bierstadt's summit. The reason? A half dozen trails meandered into thick groves of willows that dropped from the 11,600 feet pass to 11,000 feet or so in the vale between us and the base of the summit. We decided to bushwhack our way through, sometimes feeling like Humphrey Bogart aboard the African Queen in search of the main channel of the Bora river to Lake Victoria. Just when we thought we found a way, the willows thickened up. George, wearing alpine short pants, fell into a hollow and almost disappeared completely. By the time we got to him, he had already managed to pull himself up on his feet while laughing all the time. Realizing that he was not hurt, we chimed in.

At the bottom of the vale some five or six hundred feet lower than the pass, we forded a stream, sunk ankle deep in subalpine marshes, and backtracked several times around incredibly thick clumps of willows. We forged up the willowy base of Bierstadt until we arrived, at last, on relatively free tundra at perhaps 12,000 feet. Grays and Torreys had nothing like this. They seemed relatively simple in comparison.

Willy and I stopped frequently to photograph flowers and to catch our breath. Willy coined a name for the Russian thistles coating the side of the mountain. He called them eclipse flowers because they looked just like a bunch of miniature dark eclipses with the sun behind them. Between the spiny thistles grew bight-red Indian paintbrushes, and down in hollows of rock, cluster of miniature columbines helped create a tundra palette with colors enough for the western artist Jacob Alfred Miller or Albert Bierstadt himself. A circular cluster of crusty green lichens a foot and a half in diameter coated the side of a rock and looked quite literally like an artist's palette. Such a growth could easily be 150 years old and serves as a base camp for future mosses which in turn collect dusts and soils. Perhaps a few hundred years from now tundra flowers and dwarf willows will be sprouting from this rock.

Willy tapped me on the shoulder and said to look around. I had been so involved with the tundra before me that I had failed to notice how high we had climbed. To the west, in dark shadows, rose the twin-like peaks of Grays and Torreys. On the day we climbed them, Torryes looked far more rugged than Grays, but from this distant perspective we could see the jagged south-facing side of Grays, which clearly matched the rugged north-facing slope of the Torreys, the side we had been exposed to during our ascent 12 days ago.

To the southwest we could make out the peaks of the Collegiate Range but our view to the east was still blocked by the ever-rising slope of Bierstadt. George and Ike rested on rocks a hundred yards or so beyond us looking like two alpine mammals of some sort so much did they blend in with space. Ike and Father George continually discussed the existence of God, Ike being the doubter. Father George could not have had better props to argue in God's favor than the sublimity of an immense alpine panorama surrounding and dwarfing us all.

After frequent stops for catching our breath and admiring close up the "eclipse" thistles with heads bent downslope and minute clusters of purple phlox, we caught up with Ike and George at the saddle between a false summit and Mount Bierstadt looming ever upward. Here we could finally see the massive tundra-clad Mount Evans rising to the east and a deep rocky gorge beneath us serving as an echo chamber for the high-pitched squeaking of tiny rabbit-like pikas scampering on lower ledges. We estimated that we stood at about 13,000 feet.

Willy ran up to George and Ike, and all three plodded steadily ahead, slowly putting distance between themselves and me. My friends were out of sight and thunder began to rattle. Rock slabs rose above, but I sensed that I was arriving at that point where land is mostly sky.

My friends stood awaiting my arrival. I waved a weary hello and walked over to the summit's northern edge to peer down several thousand feet into a rugged glacial cirque gleaming with dark lakes. Thunder boomed all around and the skies were darkened dangerously. But the sun shone down on us. Father George said rather whimsically that if the Red Sea parted for Moses...A mixture of rain and snow zoomed in on us while lightning bolts danced not too far away. We wanted a photograph of us taken by the camera set to click in 30 seconds. After grabbing the camera, we dashed down the trail to a rocky shelter where we ate lunch.

Mount Bierstadt lived up to its name. As we sat huddled between 13,000 and 13,500 feet, torrents of rain and lightening etched the sky to the south while an equally impressive storm zeroed in on the nearby mountains to the north. Bearing down on us from the west came a third storm. But where we sat the sun beamed down as though we had been placed in the canvas of a great Bierstadt mountainscape.

We feasted on a communal lunch. Willy sliced his garden-fresh zucchini squash. I split my delicatessen feta cheese, George shaved his spicy salami and Ike peeled his oranges. Willy served as the assembly plant. We ate faster than Willy's hands could move, but he continued to produce satisfying morsels until we had stuffed ourselves. There was enough left over to feed several other mountaineers. Father George paralleled our 13,000-foot feast with Christ's multiplication of loaves. The principle of sharing multiplied tenfold the joy of hungry men eating, which in turn dissipated fears of inevitable storms.

We got up on our stiff legs and picked up a clearly marked trail that dropped off at an almost dangerous pitch down to the valley of willows. We didn't want to get blasted by lightening and made a quick descent. Within an hour we thrashed our way through willows dampened by rain. I looked up at Bierstadt covered in mist and cloud. It looked higher than Mount Everest from this willow jungle below.

I couldn't imagine a better way to have intensified our lives than these few hours above the din of daily travail.

Omak Before the Thunder

Cattle low and lie down on the earth
one at a time as clouds gather rain and sag
in the distance like sacks of cracked rye.

Torn gray rain, like shredded laughing,
curves with the wind and falls. Below,
sage resonates a blue scent, a bass note: an echo.

Something wise, but borrowed, reminds us
that a hat will stop no amount of weather,
reminds us that this is how stubborn ones die.

The cattle have known it since before the first gust
and slide their jaws indifferently as the first drops
wet their short hair and the grass above them.

An ear twitches, a dog barks, something draws
the sage further up the arete. With a short nod
and a silent response, we coil our ropes and go.

— T. R. Peterson
Flagstaff, Arizona

One Day

I walked with my friend
along the high spine of the mountains—
that beautiful bitter edge—
all the clouds and the round world
now lower than my feet.
I should have known better—
stepping down the yielding froth
of early-season snow
as clean as sugar.
I heard the thunder first
and wondered, but everything began
the terrible jiggling—
everything, I say:
the whole locomotive of winter—
nothing solid
but a maw of snow
sucking my feet.
"This is it," I thought;
and I watched,
each moment expecting
Now? Or now?
The sky sunk upward.
Then mountains of silence.

I could see some bleary crystalled light;
my right forearm waved in the air.

Years later I learned
my friend had looked
and looked

and looked
and almost left
but looked again.
I remember my one free hand
clawing for my nose.
I remember calling out.

Getting down from there to timberline
was larceny: stealing elevation
from the jaws of avalanches.
One pair of skis between us now.
Wet and cold.
No trail. And losing daylight.
We crashed through willow thickets
knee-deep in snow,
and found the road
just before we would have lost
our hands in front of us to darkness.

Though like most of us,
I think I know what happens next
from day to day,
sometimes a moment blazes like a diamond
and everything is as it is
and holy,
swaying from a dark stem.

— Chris Hoffman
Boulder, Colorado

Peak Scar Owls

Tree roots send their seepage stains
down the white walls of silence.
Late November, Christmas creeping
into the corners of the mind
and the day wanting to be dark
early. Mud and snackpot cartons,
climbers fouling their nest as
Birdland, Wings and *Ornithology*
suggest other nests were fouled.
Steep cracks and sharp breaks must wait
for this film of greasy glaze
to be freeze-dried on the other side
of the slowly turning solstice.
A flock of kamakazi pheasants
shriek off the clifftop to crash
somewhere below. Only a wren
is alarmed. Back on the road above
I have lost the will to leave.
And then the owls start calling
across the valley, looping
scattered woods. I join in and bring
one close. We talk a long time
into the night, almost relieving
a drab unclimbing Saturday.

— Terry Gifford
Sheffield, England

The Devil's Slide, Lundy Island

Cliffs stood like splintered bones
sliced by that slab-shaft of light,
a red rock-ray of Lundy sunset.

Below, a dark sea shifted, lapped,
as oil spill sludge sucked and tongued
caves and zawns towards the night.

But sitting in that last cooling glow
of achievement, they had escaped
the pull of night and sea and gravity

on *The Devil's Slide.* Their toes had seen
what their tongues could have tasted–
the salted grains of granite angled

for an *Angel's Uplift*, rather, onto
this moorland strip on an enchanted ship,
this horizon adrift among horizons.

— Terry Gifford
Sheffield, England

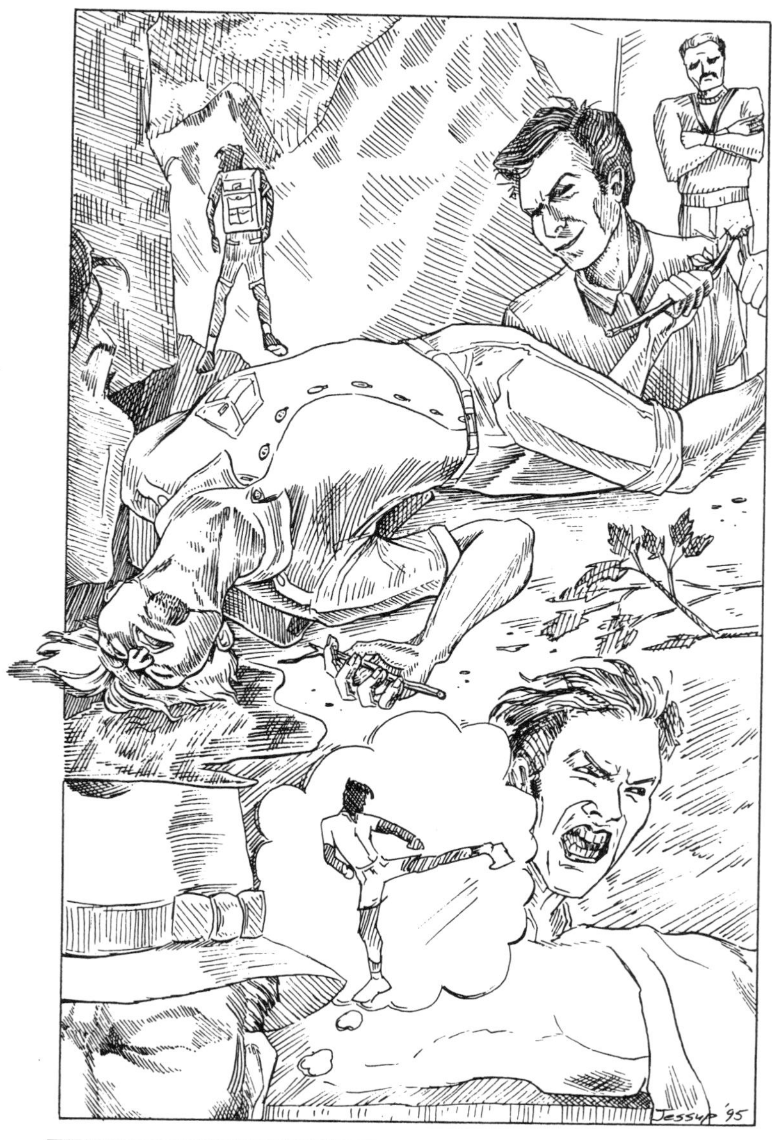

The Apparent Cause — Pen and ink drawing by Susan Jessup

The Apparent Cause

of his fall was inattention.
Waldrop, his companion on the expedition,
says Stickley looked back over his left shoulder
to emphasize a point
and put his right foot over the edge.
I phoned Wittenburg, Stickley's usual partner.
He was skeptical about Waldrop's explanation.
He cried out 'You might as well imagine
him fighting bulls in Madrid.
He never did anything dangerous. Never.'
Wittenburg, also a botanist, hadn't come over this year
because his daughter was getting married
in the middle of the summer season.
He said Stickley would not have been talking
at all while hiking single-file.
That it annoyed him not to be able to hear
or make himself heard,
and on a ledge he would never
have taken his eyes off the path.
If Stickley had to cross a cliff for a specimen
he would, but if you had insulted his mother
while he was crossing,
he would not have turned around
till he was in the meadow.

Wittenburg said he had advised Stickley
not to take Waldrop. Waldrop had called
the trip "stick collecting with Stickley,"
which to Wittenburg showed a lack of respect
for both scientist and science. He thought
Stickley could easily have found

someone more congenial, perhaps a student,
but Stickley was gay and avoided students.

Wittenburg called me back next day
wondering if Waldrop's pretense
of not being interested
could have been a smoke-screen
hiding a strong desire to go,
a way of concealing premeditation.
He suggested that we double-check the body
for signs of a blow or kick. He said
Waldrop is too choleric Just
to push someone off a cliff.

This is a model of the ledge and the drop
and the position of the body, so you can get
a good idea of the incident. Yes, I carved it
myself. It helps me to visualize. I find
I can't solve crimes using photographs.
This is where he supposedly set his foot on the air.
He might have, if he hadn't seen
that the cliff, and the ledge with it,
was about to veer to the left,
but the turn had been in view for at least three meters.
The autopsy showed several fractured vertebrae,
one in the neck and others lower down.
All that damage was consistent
with such a fall, and he landed on his back,
on the right side of his back, to be precise,
so his backpack might nave been responsible,
not Waldrop, for the fractures. Wittenburg's

suggestion did make me think of karate, though,
and I questioned the cowherds. If they had
seen anything they would have come forward.
When I talked with them I asked if they had
heard anything. They told me that they had,
a peculiar yell, and they reproduced it.
It was a karate yell. I reread the autopsy,
and it listed a deep bruise on the left
buttock not explainable by the way
Stickley struck the ground. In other words,
the ground there was more or less flat
and without rocks. So Wittenburg may
be right.

What we would like you to do
in England is find out if Waldrop ever studied
martial arts, and also if Wittenburg had it
in for Waldrop, or if either of them had it
in for Stickley. If any of the players carried
some old enmity, some unexpressed anger that has
backed up over time. If a crash in Stickley's work
could have furthered their careers in any
substantial way, or if any of them was riding
an aggression escalator. We are determined
to prosecute, because we do not want foreigners
to think of the Bavarian Alps as safe for murder.

— Elizabeth N. Evasdaughter
Raleigh, North Carolina

The Edge

A new reach for me
two weeks across the Sierra
alone with a top map
beyond man's trash
all high places off trails.

Restless on my last afternoon
couldn't wait until next morning
I would race daylight to find my truck.

From a high ridge
I dropped down a chimney
skirted a glacier
on the edge of a sheer cliff
danced and slid down five thousand feet
over rocks and boulders
into a freezing lake.

It was dark
I was cold-wet
bruised and tired
when 1 found my truck.

1 was the only one
who knew where 1 was
or where I had been.

— Clair Killen
Jacksonville, Oregon

If Death Ever Becomes Desirable

I will remember
that I came to these mountains
alone for two days,

that nothing mattered
but trees and sky,
forest's endless pine breath,
a final cold taste
in the mountain's mouth fading
at the start of summer,

that I awoke in the night
to watch a sugary sky
spill while I slept,

that insects scribbled
their hour-long lives
in fast motion over sunny air,
trying to get in as many circles
as possible
before death stalled them.

— Kathryn de Leon
Whittier, California

Half Dome

On the mist trail, early,
stone stairs
climbing dark into dark.

Vernal Fall a sound, no more,
a presence beside us, fine
spray confusing our breath.

Powder of stars pouring past,
thick, pale, shrinking
in cold
of dawn, October.

First light, and cairns
leading though manzanita,
a lost lake, oak and willow
yellowing under sugar pine.

Slabs begin, narrowing ledges,
and then the intimate terrace
of sand where rope comes free,
unloosened like hair from shoulders.

Fingertips, toes tighten across
the granite—roof, ramp,
crack, dike—curving spine
of stegosaurus immersed
in rock. Rope recoils
in high-perched trough,
onion layers slipping
away. Walk then, pitched

up into circle of snows
where all is written
afternoon. Walk, wander,
only rock, what need another
half, so entirely huge
and whole, one
world of stone, connect
momentarily with feet,
then sky, sky, sky, sky.

— Paul Willis
Carpinteria, California

Espiritu Canyon

Espiritu Canyon is around the back of the Rincon Mountains,
the range the Papago called the Turkey Necks,
where they sent their women to give birth.
To get there you have to four wheel drive for miles,
not on the southern road which goes past the petroglyphs,
winding around the cave which legend says
is filled with bandits gold,
but around the north end, beyond the ruins of the stagecoach stop.
You go that way for a long time,
past the deep pools of Tanque Verde Falls
where drunken cliff divers end up in splattered heaps,
past the turn for The Chute and Cheevah Falls,
where trucks and jeeps end up in splattered heaps.

The road to Espiritu is unmarked, unnoticed,
usually taken by no one except ranchers.
Along that road a cattle pond appears unexpectedly
reminding me of the monster in Quitobaquito Lake.
Quitobaquito is dried up now but the legend remains
of the giant sea beast who used to live there,
back in the days when the Hohokam hunted mastodon.

When my grandfather was young
someone found three fossil teeth in the dry Quitobaquito mud,
each fang nearly twelve inches long.
The reflection of Reef of Rocks and Rincon Peak
shimmer across the surface of the cattle pond
and I hope that someone remembered to put a sea monster in there.

The gate to Espiritu Canyon is closed
and we are forced to walk the last stretch

across the bedrock of the narrow gorge
where oasis alternates with waterfall
and the ash and cottonwood display a secret taste of autumn,
hidden here long after winter has set in everywhere else.
When the wind blows
it sends ripples ricocheting across the pools,
deep granite waterbasins disturbed momentarily
by the tiny waves racing atop the surface.

In the soft sand perfect for camping,
there are plenty of footprints, deer, javelina, bobcat,
bird, and fox. I search for coyote tracks,
The Hopi have a legend that when time has ended
the footprints of Coyote will be the last to disappear
I believe also that the last footprints the coyote leaves
will be ripples from walking on water in Espiritu Canyon.

— Gary Every
Tuscon, Arizona

Descending From the Top of the World

Pay attention on your descent from the top
of the world out of the alpine
where the battered saxifrage find a spot
in the tundra and claim their place;
eventually, the frail, pioneering pine
frame the scene and sound a welcome note
for the ear weary of wind,
the eye drugged with too much view.

There, improbably, in a protected defile
at a certain turn in the trail
among the rocks, columbine
give off a porcelain glow
of creamy lobes, icy sepals,
and darker petal spurs beautifully composed.
Tethered with the thinnest stems
the blossoms seem to float above the rock
like dreams, those supreme fictions,
no less believable for seeming real.

— J. J. McKenna
Omaha, Nebraska

The Gendarme

by Ralph Mitchell

In an obscure corner of West Virginia, near the triangular intersection of state routes 28, 55, and 33, stands a unique climbing store. Few of the people passing by on the nearby road are aware of its presence. Like the mythical city of Shangri-La, it exists beyond the realm of the casual traveler. To find The Gendarme takes purpose. Tucked away behind Buck Harper's General Store and the Rocks View Restaurant, its construction mimics the local small barns and outbuildings. The siding consists of rough-sawn boards nailed vertically, and the cracks in between are covered with coarse battens. The silver steel roof is the Gendarme's most prominent feature. The raised ribs run the length of it, from the spouting to the ridge, and provide a sense of purpose to the structure that is lost among the rest of its components. One small window on the side and the door in front permit a meager amount of natural light into the interior. Faded with age and almost hidden from view behind the branches of a small tree, a sign hangs from a pole and announces the name of the store.

The porch is cluttered with an odd assortment of chairs and benches An aluminum lawn chair, its nylon seat hanging in tatters, sits next to a log bench suspended from four crooked legs of various diameters. Its top hewn flat almost as an after thought. The porch posts are tied together with a worn wooden railing that must be used as seating also. Ashtrays are strewn haphazardly about. Some perch like chickens on the railing. Others hunker down among the jetsam strewn about the floor. In the center, an old cable reel, battered, burned, carved, and stained, presides over the collection. The remnants of someone's snack still adorn its top. Pushed back against the wall to the left of the door, sits a six-foot-long corroded aluminum box. Stenciled on the front are the words: "For Emergency Use Only Stokes

Litter." Covering the top of the box are bundles of firewood, neatly bound and labeled "$3." A large bulletin board is handily fastened to the wall above the firewood. Covering its face are a multitude of notes, advertisements, and Park Service notices. One note reads: "To whom it may concern: Wasp nest located above the crux of Soler, use caution if climbing this route." Another offers climbing shoes for sale "cheap." A third, tattered and faded, makes one wonder if Jennifer ever did meet Steve at the base of Old Man's route. A Park Service notice, advising of cliff closures due to the Peregrine Falcon nesting season, hangs off to the right. Immediately to the right of the notice is the door.

Once inside, a person is struck by the incredible amount of climbing paraphernalia clinging to the walls and counters. Toward the back of the store, a collection of used and outdated equipment hangs from the wall. In any other sport, they would reside in a Hall of Fame or a museum: an icon behind glass to be revered, out of touch to all. But here they typify the innocence of the sport, where the pioneers and the legends remain accessible to even the meekest among their brethren.

Holding court behind the cash register stands John Markwell, purveyor of fine climbing gear and finer advice. The twinkle in his eye as he talks to a customer reveals the nature of someone who truly enjoys what he is doing. A head of graying hair seems to be his only concession to the passing years. His trim, athletic build speaks of someone years younger. He started his business out of the back of a Volkswagen bus in the mid-60s. He was a brilliant visionary, or damned lucky, as few foresaw the dramatic growth of the sport in the subsequent years. He lives in a fine brick home, one of the seven or eight that comprise the little community, several doors back up the road. After living there for over twenty years, he is still regarded with suspicion by the locals. His children, however, participate fully as members of the community.

Toward dusk, the climbers begin filtering into the parking area across the street from Harper's General Store. Stepping gingerly over a flattened rattlesnake, they pause then continue down the community's only alley onto the porch of the Gendarme where they settle into whatever seating is still available. One climber, wearing brightly colored clothing and a rebellious haircut, stands talking animatedly. His arms gesticulate wildly. Another sits in a chair tipped back against the wall, hands folded across his chest, and eyes with apparent amusement the rest of the group. None is a permanent resident of the area. Most are from towns and cities all over the eastern United States, and several have traveled from the West and other countries as well. They are drawn here by the nearby climbing and the opportunity to renew old friendships and establish new ones.

The conversation begins as an anarchic free-for-all then gradually forms into a common subject, with everyone offering his or her own insight. The topics could include anything, from yesterday's epic climbs to tomorrow's projects, from the terminal ballistics of the newly adopted FBI .40 caliber sidearm to the amount of guano produced by a pet iguana in a week. As the night turns to early morning, the group reluctantly disbands and returns to tents to pass the remainder of the night in relative quiet.

Previous generations each laid claim to an edifice to serve as a focal point for their social interaction. In today's age of car phones and faxes, social boundaries no longer are defined by physical limits but by common interests and goals. The Gendarme stands as a contemporary version of a social center point for one small segment of society: The Climbing Community.

Philosophy of the Rock

by Louis Komjathy

The philosophy of the rock recognizes the elemental importance of wildness for spiritual and psychological health. It rejects the unquestioning acceptance of a domination paradigm (mountains to be conquered, summits to be claimed, routes to be forged into rock cliffs) by many climbers. The philosophy of the rock does not simply look at granite and sandstone formations as aesthetically pleasing aspects of the landscape, but rather sees an explanation of interconnectedness within nature's endowing complexity. To climb a rock is not a struggle with or an overcoming of the uprising pinnacle. The pathless activity involves a struggle not with the rock, but with one's own fears, frustrations, anxieties and disappointments. It is to rise above one's self to discover the true emergence of possibility. The journey within an elevated climb is to understand, to experience, the interrelation between an individual and the Earth's myriad life forms. Moving within a heightened organic peak, one finds familial communion with the birth of rivers and the recollection of glacial movements. To love the beauty and feel the presence of life's extending contours, this is the philosophy of the rock, the mystery of the mountains. It is a passionate wilderness experience that realizes the essential significance of a preservation imperative for ecological awareness—an expression of hope for the continuing contribution of mountain and forested-valley poetry. To place one's hands within the perfection of a water-polished rock fissure, to rest upon a thousand-foot ledge, is to know a sense of place. It is to feel the oneness through the depth of one's being. The subterranean harmony of nature's evolution proclaims unity in a spatial expanse—revealing how the hand is an extension of the rock, how the rock articulates a life anticipating hidden discovery. This is the *practice* of the rock. This is the secret deep within.

The Boardman Tasker Memorial Award

Founded as a memorial to Peter Boardman and Jo Tasker, two able mountaineering writers who were los attempting the unclimbed Noth-East Ridge of Everest in 1982, the award of £2,000 is made to the book judged to be of most outstanding quality in each year.

Since 1984 the Award has been made every year, and has included among the winners much mountain-relted non-fiction including Jim Perrin's *Menlove*, Joe Simpson's best-selling *Touching the Void*, Doug Scott and Alex MacIntyre's *The Shishapangma Expedition*, Stephen Venables' *Painted Mountains*, and Victor Saunders' *Elusive Summits*. A notable recent development has been awards to fiction titles including Alison Fell's Mer de Glace, John M. Harrison's The Climbers, and Jeff Long's The Ascent in 1993, and increasing interest from North American Publishers and writers.

Liveliness in the judging panel is maintained by a two-year term of office, and the juxtaposition each year of three judges with varied interests.

The Award enjoys a healthy entry of more than twenty books a year and promotes discussion and interest in all entries. It seeks to promote continued good writing on mountaineering, which already has a fine tradition stretching back to the Victorian era.

Eligibility for the Award is limited to books distributed in the United Kingdom.

Following is the list of finalists:

- ✓ *The Burgess Book of Lies* by Adrian and Alan Burgess
- ✓ *K2 The Story of the Savage Mountain* by Jim Curran
- ✓ *Vertical Pleasure* by Mick Fowler
- ✓ *Geoffrey Winthrop Young* by Alan Hankinson
- ✓ *Everest Calling* by Lorna Siggins

The Burgess Book of Lies

***The Burgess Book of Lies* by Adrian & Alan Burgess**
EXCERPT (PAGE 82)—DEATH OF A SHERPA: TO A LOST FRIEND BY ALAN BURGESS
ISBN 0/938 567/38/1 $30 463pp
United States: Cloudcap Publishing, Seattle; (206) 365-9192
Canada: Rocky Mountain Books, Calgary; (403) 249-9490
United Kingdom: (distributed by Cordee) (1116) 2543579

Death of a Sherpa: To a Lost Friend

by Alan Burgess

Looking upward, I saw a body splayed horizontal, with out-stretched arms windmilling and clawing at empty air. My Sherpa climbing partner, Ongchu, was falling, caught in time and space, his face twisted, already resigned to death.

The vision vanished. I saw the *real* Ongchu balanced 100 feet above, linked to me by an eight-millimeter nylon rope as I stood vulnerable and unprotected on an ice step, with the slope dropping away to a deep crevasse 600 feet below. Unusually nervous and distracted by the premonition, I screwed an ice piton into the slope and tied into it, even though I knew that should Ongchu fall, it would rip immediately from the ice.

The rope ran smoothly through my hands and shards of ice tinkled past me, loosened by Ongchu's boots. He disappeared from sight, moving quickly on easier ground, climbing to find a good anchor point for the fixed line. Nothing but a slight breeze and flickering rays of light disturbed my isolation. There was crystal silence and the quiet rhythm of my heart beating.

The faint sound of crampon steel crunched on ice, and an urgent cry cut to my core. My muscles responded as if hit by a high-voltage current. In a terrifying *déjà-vu,* my eyes witnessed what my heart already knew. Ongchu was falling, his body stretched across the ice. Grasping at air, his glove flew away and his red jacket caught a flicker of light. He swept by a mere arm's length to my left, his stare frozen, a scream cut short by a glancing blow to the head. Bouncing down a sharp craggy rock wall, his body flew into the void, before crashing and spinning onto the ice and then plunging with a sickening thud onto the slope below. A streak of blood led to a small bundle which had halted in deep powder snow where the slope eased. Nothing moved.

It was October 31, 1990. I was 200 feet from the Tibetan border on a mountain called Cheo Himal in the central Nepalese Himalaya. My friends and climbing companions, John and Matt, were 300 feet below, silent witnesses to the fragility of life.

Although we had started out as clients and guide, our relationship had become much closer than that. We all came from my home village of Holmfirth, and this expedition had forged strong bonds among us, as mountains have a way of doing. Now we were to share something else that mountains can produce: tragedy. Trembling with shock, I glanced down at the tiny broken figure that was once a proud Sherpa. I thought . . . dead.

Above 20,000 feet and balanced on an ice step in one of the farthest corners of the world is not a place to panic. Fighting down terror and feelings of lightness and floating sensations, I breathed deeply and slowly until I regained physical and emotional control. I knew I had to descend, but I also understood that the slightest lack of concentration could result in my own death.

I rappelled slowly, resisting the urge to hurry back to my companions. They appeared calmer than I, and after talking myself through how to descend, I continued on down.

Jumping across the deep crevasse at the foot of the slope,

I landed in thigh-deep powder snow and plunged on down towards Ongchu's body, following the trail of blood and disturbed snow. The body moved and struggled to sit up. Ongchu was still alive! Gasping for air, I reached him and quickly scanned his head and limbs in an attempt to assess his injuries. Blood seeped from a hole in his temple the size of an egg, and he coughed up frothy red spumes from his lungs. One eye was smashed and closed, while the other flickered with desperation and fear. His limbs all seemed intact, almost a miracle as I thought back to the series of thuds his body had made on the ice.

As I watched John and Matt approach, my gaze continued past them to the looming ice cliff that threatened us. If the cliff—the size of a hotel—collapsed, we all would be crushed instantly. I screamed at them to hurry and then apologized. They understood only too well the urgency of the situation and smoothly followed my instructions to cross the slope to the left to escape the threat.

Leaving Ongchu, who was now groaning in agony, I hurried after them and anchored a rope that led to safety 300 feet lower. It was Matt's first day on an alpine ice climb, and even though he demonstrated natural climbing talent, I was reluctant to involve him in additional danger. John, who had already summited a 20,000-foot peak with me the previous year, had considerable experience on alpine terrain and could be trusted to get them both onto safer ground. I told them to wait on the glacier for me, and I watched them head down the rope.

Terrified of the leaning ice cliffs, and even more frightened of the decisions I was being forced to make, I traversed back across the ice to Ongchu to see what could be done.

He lay on his side in the fetal position, moaning softly. His hat and gloves were lost during his fall, and he was beginning to shake from shock and cold. Slowly easing his body around, I managed to get him into a sitting position and pulled my own wool hat onto his head. Resting his head against the snow had stopped the bleeding from the large hole in his skull, but pulling gloves onto his swollen and wooden hands was difficult. His head lolled against my shoulder as I supported him.

"Sorry, sir." A dry moan—half mumble, half pain—whispered from his lips.

"Ongchu! Ongchu!" I said. "Can you hear me?"

His one clear eye moved with signs of recognition.

"We're going down, Ongchu! Down! Can you hear me?"

With a shudder that seemed to come from the very core of his soul, he tensed and made as if to stand. The courage that has endeared the Sherpa people to all mountaineers radiated from him.

His limbs did not appear broken, and he struggled to straighten his legs as I hoisted him to a standing position. How would my courage have stood the test if the situation were reversed?

Suddenly, as if a light had been switched off, the power drained from him, and he slumped back into the snow. I tried again to raise him, but he was too heavy and he curled onto his side. I glanced up at the lengthening shadows on the ice cliff and tried to believe it would not collapse.

I realized it was impossible to take him down the way we had climbed. It was too steep and crevassed. The only possibility was to go directly down the slope under the ice cliff and hope there were no obstacles that proved impassable. I tied a length of rope to his harness and plunged through thigh-deep powder snow. Dragging Ongchu through the snow, I managed to move him only ten feet before he dug in his heels. He was shouting with pain. The harness tugging on his body must have aggravated some internal injury, plus disturbing possibly broken ribs.

Panting heavily, I climbed back up my trail, tears of sorrow and frustration flooding my cheeks. Unsure of what to do next, I traversed back across the ice to the point where our fixed line dropped away over steep crevassed ice. I knew I could never take Ongchu down that way. It was beginning to dawn on me there was little chance of rescue. Even if I could get him down the 400 feet to the glacier, base camp was still 1,500 feet lower, and medical help many days away.

I trudged once more back to my friend. He was very still, but I could hear him breathing rapidly. I squatted on my haunches with my back to the mountain and looked south to the massive bulk of Manaslu. Memories flooded back from our expedition there the previous October, and I could see clearly the point of our final camp and remembered the fearful night Aid and I had spent battling hurricane-force winds. Now it was calm, and the late autumn sun bounced long shadows and sharp rays of light across the ice.

Waves of emotion surged over me. The stark wild beauty of this place contrasted with the warm vulnerable body lying at my side. Yet here was the balance of nature at its most Spartan and everything was in its place. Even death has its reasons. I felt resigned to the outcome: Ongchu was going to die.

My gaze dropped to the snow, and tears of sadness glazed my vision. I struggled to come to terms with my decisions and actions. Maybe I had sent my two companions down too soon? Maybe with their help we could have dragged Ongchu farther down the slope? But suppose we had even got him as far down as the glacier, what then? His head injuries were massive, and without the help that only a hospital can give, he would die anyway. Suppose I had insisted that we all stay together and the sérac had collapsed, killing all four of us! Was it worth the risk? The voices of self-critical demons rang in my ears. But all speculation was irrelevant. All I could do was to deal with the immediate situation.

My memory drifted back to the first time I'd met Ongchu in the streets of Kathmandu, surrounded by the bells of rickshaws, the shouting of street vendors, the smells of open markets and the warm autumn sunshine of early October. Another Sherpa friend had known I was looking to hire a strong climbing Sherpa to help with the expedition and had recommended Ongchu. On meeting him, I knew instantly what a competent climber he would prove to be. Like many of the best climbing Sherpas, in the lowlands he was reserved to the point of shyness but carried a strong barrel chest and compact body with confidence and pride. When I asked him which mountains he had climbed, he looked me straight in the eye and listed a string of high peaks, including a recent K2 expedition. He didn't boast; he simply stated his experience.

Later that day, when I introduced him to the climbing team, I voiced my opinion that the closer to the mountain and the high valleys we got, the more capable he would become. His reserve would evaporate in his more familiar terrain of rock walls and glistening ice fields.

On the "walk-in," he blended easily with the Sherpa cook staff and was always searching for ways to help, whether in the kitchen, putting up tents or dealing with porters. On the mountain, I considered him my equal, not only in climbing strength, but in route-finding and decision-making. We had planned the final assault together and had taken turns leading the steep ice on the climb.

The day we reached base camp, Ongchu and I raced ahead of the main group to look for a good campsite. He spoke little and when he did, it was always deferentially. He called me "sir," which I found unfamiliar. With most of my Sherpa friends, I always joked around, laughing and telling stories, drinking *chang* with them and teasing the pretty girls along the trails. I wondered if Ongchu's shyness with me was partially the result of the kitchen Sherpas' talk; our *sirdar* had been on Everest with the Canadians in 1982 when he was a first-time expedition Sherpa and I was acting climbing leader. Ongchu may have regarded me as some wealthy big-time expedition leader with the potential to hire him on a continual basis. Regardless of his shyness, when it came to matters of mountains, he was both confident and assertive. Some of my best and longest-term friends had taken quite a while to get to really know.

Desperation made me try once again to lift Ongchu. I shouted into his face and turned him over onto his back. A great sigh hissed from his lungs and he shook his head heavily from side to side. He reached down, flung his gloves to the ice and untied the rope from his harness. He had decided not to be painfully hauled around any more but to spend his last moments in the way he chose.

I followed the trail once more to the top of the fixed rope. I thought this time I would leave and force myself to go on down. I lifted the rope to attach it to my harness, and then I stopped. If I could not save Ongchu, then it was important to me how he died. If he felt abandoned, I would always feel guilty and would never know about those last minutes. I dropped the rope and turned back across the ice.

I crouched by his silent body and stared out across the valley. If a person had to die, there was no place more beautiful. Better to slip away here than in some hospital bed weighed down by tubes, blinded by fluorescent light and asphyxiated by the smell of antiseptic. The cold provides its own anesthetic, and while the bodily pain becomes numbed, the mind must still be aware of this brilliant light and deep powerful silence.

After ten or fifteen minutes, Ongchu began to stir again. He half turned and I helped rise to a sitting position. The effort to hold his head up proved too much, and it hung exhausted on his chest. I knew that, like all Sherpa people, Ongchu was a devout Buddhist, and the process of his death was of utmost importance to him. I recalled the stages of dying from *The Tibetan Book Of The Dead*: when a Buddhist *lama* talks to the dying person, literally walking him through the final stages of life and into the state prior to rebirth. My memory of the text was a little rusty, but I figured the process of dying must be the same for everyone.

I spoke softly and as calmly as I could. I told Ongchu not to be afraid, that I was his brother and would be there with him when he started to slip away into the long tunnel with a bright light at the end. I realized I was speaking as much for myself as for him, but hoped he would trust me. I told him not to fight the flow towards the light but to concentrate on it and feel himself as part of that light. I urged him not to be distracted by sounds or shadows but to focus his inner vision on the white glow; to feel the warmth of that light and let it absorb him.

I let his body rest back on the snow, not knowing how far away from death he was. Staring out across the lower valleys, I tried hard to remember what came next and how far I could go with him. A cold wind was freshening and clouds swirled around the high ridges, mixing blasts of powder and streaks of air.

My gaze returned to Ongchu's still form. Mumbling half to myself, I spoke into the rising wind:

"When the white light turns to a red glow and begins to fade, have courage, don't be scared. The darkness will change again to light. Then it's up to you, my friend. Where you're at now, you know better than me."

I felt very human and vulnerable, but I also felt weightless, as if I could almost fly. Maybe death is not so bad. Only the fear and pain of it? I felt that now was the time to go. There was a quiet peace in the air, and I rose to leave.

With a last long stare, seeing only a shape, I turned firmly away and forced myself to keep moving without any backward glance. I took a strong hold on the fixed line and slid over the edge, down the ice, through crevasses and across snow bridges, down to John and Matt.

The three of us regrouped on the edge of a bottomless chasm. We stood in silence and turned to start on down the glacier. Now was not the time or place to explain all the thoughts and actions of the last three hours. Communication was restricted to safety commands and route-finding, as we circled large crevasses and leapt across smaller ones.

I looked upward searching for the body and saw a black crow circling, cruising the rising air. Did I see a black speck move high on the face? My eyes played tricks and my mind jumped around like a kite in a storm. We pressed on down toward our camp.

Our Sherpa kitchen staff had seen only three people returning and, with an intuition born of experience, already suspected the worse. Tired and dejected, we staggered into camp. The expedition was over, and an avalanche would shortly wipe out all trace of our passing.

Two of our kitchen boys were lay monks, and that night they lit candles, burnt juniper and intoned prayers so that Ongchu's spirit could find its way down from the mountain. They believe it is important the spirit knows that the body is dead and that it's time to move on to its next reincarnation.

Now that the expedition was over, we left the stark frozen base camp and descended into the forests, wandering through the warm lower meadows rich with autumn colours. Small streams trickled into rivers that foamed under rough wooden bridges, and fallen leaves formed carpets of rust and ochre. The sound of small birds calling merrily pierced the quiet, while sunbeams filtered through hanging mosses that looked like old men's beards. We strode down the trail through a valley made more magical by contrast with the high places we had left only that morning. We needed to know we were alive and breathed in large lungfuls of joy with primitive passion.

With the passage of time, the emotion of that experience has dimmed, partly because more recent experiences have taken precedence. Six months after the death of Ongchu, I helped rescue a young German climber from a peak in the Langtang region of Nepal. He had fallen and broken both legs below the knee, landing on a snow shelf above 20,000 feet. At first, it appeared a hopeless task, but with hard work and a little skill, we brought him to safety. It was one of the most satisfying times I ever spent on a mountain, and during that rescue I often wondered what would have happened if Ongchu had only broken his legs or had the accident occurred in a less remote area.

It would be easy to become sentimental about Ongchu and to emphasize his charming character and great personal courage, but one of the dangers with sentimentality is in the belief of "bad luck." Ongchu died because he made a mistake, and if we the living wish to continue to face dangerous situations, we must always focus on the problem at hand and not allow that concentration to waiver. The rope Ongchu was descending broke because he had untied a knot that isolated a flaw. He died because his overconfidence broke his focus, and the consequence of that was death. It was a brutal, sad lesson.

In high-standard mountaineering, many people die. Ongchu takes his place alongside many other good friends who also made mistakes. His memory still hangs around in the back of my mind, waiting for those times when I am physically or emotionally vulnerable to remind me that life is a fragile edge and only a passing phase.

K2 The Story of the Savage Mountain

***K2 The Story of the Savage Mountain* by Jim Curran**
EXCERPT (PAGE 99)—COWBOYS ON K2
ISBN 0 340 60601 0 £17.99 271pp
United Kingdom: Hodder & Stoughton Publishers (1171) 8736000
United States: The Mountaineers (206) 223-6303

Cowboys on K2

by Jim Curran

If a realistic attempt to climb K2 needed a fresh approach, what could be more appropriate than that it should come from the New World, though the driving force behind the American 1938 K2 expedition was in fact a German *émigré* from Dresden. Fritz Weissner had lived in the States since 1929 and was an American citizen. He joined the American Alpine Club in 1932 and the same year was a member of a combined German-American-Austrian expedition to Nanga Parbat. An excellent rock climber (brought up on the spectacular sandstone cliffs of the Elbe Valley), he had an impressive track record in the Alps, America and Canada, including the first ascent of Mount Waddington. In early 1937 Wiessner, with the President of the AAC, made a formal application to climb K2, but it was not until November that permission arrived for 1938. Should this attempt be unsuccessful the permit would be renewed for 1939.

Faced with the pressure of organizing a major expedition in a very short time, and having his own business commitments to cope with as well, Wiessner pulled out of the first attempt, while making it clear he wished to lead the 1939 expedition. Andy Kauffman and Bill Putnam in their excellent account *K2, the 1939 Tragedy* surmised that Wiessner may well have done this in order to let others make a first try; then in the event of failure he could take advantage of their experience. He had done this successfully before, both in Europe and on Mount Waddington. (It is perhaps also worth noting that the 1932 Nanga Parbat expedition was also the first attempt on that mountain since Mummery's ill-fated expedition in 1895. It failed, possibly reinforcing Wiessner's reluctance to do the same in 1938.) Whether a deliberate ploy or not, Wiessner recommended that the leadership should be given to Charles Houston, and with his appointment the first of the truly great climbers to be forever linked with K2 took the center stage.

Charlie Houston was then a medical student aged twenty-five. He had started his climbing career at the age of twelve in the Alps with his father. Houston admired the British climbing traditions and didn't have much use for artificial aids. He had made a number of good climbs in the Alps and had been with Washburn on Mount Crillon, Alaska. In 1934 he made the first ascent of Mount Foraker and two years later, though cruelly robbed of the summit itself through food poisoning, he was in the party which achieved the first ascent of Nanda Devi in 1936. Both these climbs had been made by small cohesive groups of close friends and in excellent style. On Nanda Devi, Houston had the temerity to invite Bill Tilman and Noel Odell of Everest fame, both well known and at the height of their powers. He was delighted that they agreed to accompany a group of almost unknown young Americans. The expedition was a model of democratic decision-making. So much so that they even planned not to release the names of any successful summiteers. In the event this proved a practical impossibility, but it did show the depth of harmony and friendship that prevailed in the team. These qualities were to be the foundation of both the 1938 expedition and again in 1953 when Houston returned to K2.

When Charlie Houston accepted the leadership from Wiessner he had not much time to pick a team and organize the expedition. His brief from the American Alpine Club was two-fold, to make a complete reconnaissance of the mountain and only then attempt to climb it. Houston had no hesitation in choosing Robert H. Bates. Bob Bates was also twenty-eight, a teacher, and had been on several major expeditions to Alaska. Perhaps his most impressive effort was with Bradford Washburn: the epic traverse of the unclimbed Mount Lucania and Mount Steele ending with a 125 mile walk out during which each man lost twenty pounds in weight. Like Houston, Bob Bates espoused the self-supporting 'small is beautiful' ethos long before it became fashionable. Bill House at twenty-five was a major force in Yale Mountaineering Club and a past President. He had climbed the Devils Tower in Wyoming and Mount Waddington, both with Fritz Wiessner. W.F. Loomis who had been on Nanda Devi with Houston could not join the party but recommended Teton guide Paul Petzoldt, who among other hard climbs had been involved in a bizarre rescue of a publicity-seeking parachutist marooned on the top of Devils Tower. Petzoldt cunningly bought fifty pitons in Europe on his way to India, which were all used.

Dick Burdsall was forty-two. In 1932 he had climbed Minya Konka, a mountain actually in China but on the edge of the Tibetan Plateau. It was one of those peaks once rumoured to be the highest mountain on earth at 30,000 feet but in fact proved to be only 24,900 (7590m). The final team member was Captain Norman Streatfeild, a Scot based in India in the Bengal Mountain Artillery, who was to be transport officer and had already been up the Baltoro Glacier to perform the same job on Gasherbrum I (Hidden Peak) with the 1936 French expedition.

Bill Tilman, who was on his way to lead an Everest expedition chose six experienced Sherpas to travel across India from Darjeeling to join Houston. Their sirdar, or head man, was Pasang Kikuli who had been Houston's personal Sherpa on Nanda Devi and had been several times to Kangchenjunga, as well as Nanga Parbat and Everest, thus amassing more Himalayan experience than the rest of the expedition put together!

It was a happy, relaxed and efficient party that set off from Srinagar on the 300-mile approach to K2. Bob Bates, who with Charlie Houston wrote the expedition book, described with awe and humility every new vista, every novel experience and their sense of anticipation as they slowly approached the mountain. Bates also recalls early during the walk-in seeing some initials carved on water-worn rock on the banks of the Dras river: 'H.H.G.A. 1861-2-3'. Henry Haversham Godwin-Austen had obviously not been above producing his own bit of minor vandalism!

When the team reached Askole, Paul Petzoldt came down with a high fever and delirium. Houston, as the expedition doctor, stayed with him while the rest carried on. In his words, 'I hadn't a clue what was wrong. . . It was agreed that if he recovered we would try to join them; if he died, I would bury him and join them! It was scary because he was in fact very sick for three days. When we got home my consultants felt he had developed sandfly or Dengue fever.' Petzoldt did recover and he and Houston caught up the rest of the team at Urdokas.

Despite a porter strike beyond Askole, which was quickly defeated by the assurance that the climbers would simply carry their own gear and not pay the porters anything at all, the expedition reached Base Camp on 12 June. Awed by the immensity of the mountain, they decided to split up to reconnoitre the three obvious possibilities previously investigated by the Duke of Abruzzi: the North-West Ridge, North-East Ridge and the Abruzzi Spur. The North-East Ridge was quickly dismissed. The mile-long knife-edged ridge looked out of the question. But, like the duke before them, Bill House was convinced that the North-West Ridge with its favourable strata would be the best bet.

Although climbing standards had improved almost beyond recognition since 1908 and the American team had a wealth of varied experience, the slopes to the Savoia Saddle climbed by the Duke's guides in twelve hours defeated them three times, not because of any intrinsic difficulty but because of the impossibility of carrying loads up to the Saddle, They surmised that snow conditions had changed dramatically over the years, which was quite possible as they were moving on pure green ice. By the late 'thirties ten-point crampons were becoming generally accepted (with the notable exception of Scotland!) but twelve-point 'lobster claw' crampons had not yet been invented. Kicking steps on snow, or step-cutting, was to remain the standard practice for many years to come. Cutting long lines of steps on hard ice was dreaded as time consuming and dangerous. Today, given the right consistency, such ice climbing is almost relished for its speed and safety. Also porters were rarely, if ever, issued with crampons and preferred to stick to rock wherever possible, however loose and unreliable. The result was that the lines of routes in both the Alps and Himalaya were often chosen for very different reasons than they are today.

Two of the three possible routes on K2 had now been eliminated and the reconnaissance party on the Abruzzi Spur were not encouraged. Though they had not been stopped by any insurmountable difficulties, they had found it insecure and lacking safe campsites. Houston had actually found a few pieces of weathered wood on the remnants of a tent platform, marking one of the Duke of the Abruzzi's camps.

These reconnaissances had used up valuable time. It was not until 1 July that the whole team assembled at the foot of the Abruzzi Spur and committed themselves to an all-out attempt. Later they were criticized for spending so long going over old ground. Oscar Dyhrenfurth in particular questioned their judgement quite sharply. But it was part of their brief to explore and it was certainly possible that thirty years of technical advances may well have invalidated the Duke of Abruzzi's assessments. Ironically it proved to be the Abruzzi Spur itself, dismissed in 1909 for its steepness and lack of campsites, that was to prove the key.

Supplies were by now running low. Worse, a three-gallon drum of gasoline had been crushed by a boulder. Streatfeild and two porters trekked across to the old French Base Camp at the foot of Gasherbrum I, where he knew that a cache of fuel had been left. But it had long since been removed by porters from Askole who had returned after the expedition to loot anything of value (a tradition that continues to the present day).

The first 1000 metres of the Spur was dominated by the need to find safe campsites. They spent several days puzzling an intricate line through tottering rock towers and little gullies before they came upon a perfect site for Camp II in a little hollow. Above this finding a good safe site became increasingly difficult. Rotten rock and frequent stonefall made progress alarming. In particular there was an ever-present danger of the leading climbers knocking rock on those below. Camp III was particularly vulnerable and two tents scored direct hits; fortunately no one was hurt. Eventually Streatfeild and Bursdall decided to descent with three Sherpas and continue the reconnaissance, mapping and photographing. Houston, Bates, House, Petzoldt and three Sherpas continued climbing upwards. In fact of the Sherpas only Pasang Kikuli ever climbed above Camp III.

The diminished team pressed on. Petzoldt led a hard, steep pitch up an overhang. Above, easier ground led to the base of a formidable barrier, a vertical band of red rock fifty metres high. Camp IV was pitched at its foot and to Bill House and Bob Bates fell the task of climbing this, the crux of the Abruzzi Spur.

Bill house was the best rock climber of the expedition and he set off up a wide chimney that narrowed to an awkward ice-filled crack. It took him four hours of desperate effort to climb twenty-five metres. It was almost completely unprotected, with only occasional resting places. At 6700 metres it was a superb lead. In 1980 Peter Boardman, arguably Britain's best Himalayan climber at that time, climbed House's Chimney and was impressed and surprised at its technical difficulty. He thought that when it was first climbed it must have been the hardest pitch in the Himalaya. Certainly it was far harder than anything climbed on Everest in the 1920s and 1930s. Camp V was placed at the top of the Chimney only a couple of rope lengths above Camp IV.

Above Camp V lurked the Black Pyramid, a complex area of steep weathered slabs and icy gullies. While the climbing was not as hard as House's Chimney it was sustained and serious, good ledges and belays were hard to find. It took a further camp halfway up which was literally hacked out of rock and rubble, before at last on 19 July only an ice traverse barred the way to Camp VII, at 7700 metres, just 200 metres below the great snow Shoulder of K2.

At this point the four climbers paused for thought. Their position could be seen in two ways. Optimistically they were poised for a real chance of a summit attempt. They had ten days' food left and with one more camp high on the Shoulder and three days of fine weather K2 could be theirs. And yet...and yet... The weather, which had been brilliant, surely couldn't last much longer? Away to the south the monsoon clouds could be seen building up on the horizon. Should they risk being trapped so high on the mountain? Could they manage to get down in a storm?

Two factors undoubtedly influenced their decision. Houston and his team were brought up in a tradition that valued safety and caution as a priority. Gambling with your life was not on. They were climbing for fun, not for fame and glory. The second factor was the original brief: to reconnoitre the mountain and, if possible, make an attempt on the summit. Psychologically it would have been hard for them suddenly to adopt the ruthless determination needed to climb K2 when they had already fulfilled most of their hopes and expectations. At its simplest, they were probably not quite psyched up enough to go for it. In the end they opted for something of a compromise. Houston and Petzoldt (chosen, as Nanda Devi, by a majority vote) would climb as high as they could on the Shoulder and examine the final summit slopes. Surely there must have been a lurking hope that, just possibly, they might achieve a bit more than that....

All four climbers, plus the indomitable Pasang Kikuli, helped establish Camp VII and on the morning of 20 July the five made it to the site just below the Shoulder. Petzoldt and Houston were left to dig out a campsite and prepare for their final effort. Then suddenly a major problem presented itself. They had somehow forgotten to bring any matches with them. Unable to melt snow, so essential for survival, their attempt would fail before it had begun. A frantic search revealed nine matches in Houston's pockets. All were unreliable and three were used to light the stove. Six were left to last the next day and following morning. They had melted enough snow to reheat in the cold light of dawn and three more matches went to make breakfast. Then, unladen with camping gear, they set off.

The Shoulder of K2 is one of the very few easy-angled areas on the whole mountain. At its lowest point it is almost flat, steepening gently before butting up against a band of rock above which a huge sérac is poised like a frozen wave about to break. Avalanche debris often litters the upper part of the Shoulder and photos of the sérac band taken over the years show marked differences as massive chunks break off. But these collapses are mercifully infrequent and although it is possible that some climbers missing on the upper slopes in later years might have been struck, there is no evidence to prove it. Nevertheless, the upper area of the Shoulder is still a dangerous place because of its altitude, and the danger of storms.

On 21 July, 1938, Petzoldt, and Houston became the first to tread the snows of the Shoulder, ploughing through waist-deep powder and making slow progress. They pressed on up its crest until just under 8000 metres Houston had enough. Petzoldt carried on for about fifty metres until he could see that there was a real chance of forcing through the rock band above him and there was what seemed to be a good, safe campsite below it. Petzoldt was now only some 600 metres from the summit which from the Shoulder seemed tantalizingly close.

Meanwhile Houston sat looking out towards Concordia about 3500 metres below him. It was a profound moment: 'I felt that all my previous life had reached a climax in these last hours of intense struggle against nature and yet nature had been very indulgent...I believe in those minutes at 26,000 feet on K2 I reached depths of feeling which I can never reach again.'

Petzoldt joined him and soon the two men descended to Camp VII in the twilight. Parched and exhausted they carefully prepared the stove and, with the very last match, it lit. Hot tea was brewed, but a cold breakfast was inevitable. In the morning, a big ring around the sun and high clouds approaching confirmed their decision to go down, though the expected storm did not arrive.

The expedition retreated safely and methodically. By any standards it had done exceptionally well, certainly achieving a lot more than most of the British Everest expeditions in the 1930s, and yet there were people who felt it should have done even better. Oscar Dyhrenfurth even suggested that had Fritz Wiessner been present the mountain might well have been climbed; a contentious argument as will be seen from the next chapter. It seems just as likely that the expedition might have torn itself apart. *Cowboys on K2*, as Charlie Houston wryly nicknames their expedition book, *Five Miles High*, remains as a superb reminder of all that is best on a harmonious expedition. Tolerance, good humour and democratic decisions have been none too common on so many subsequent K2 expeditions. *Five Miles High* should be compulsory reading for anyone contemplating going to K2, and perhaps even more so for many who have returned from the mountain at odds with themselves or their companions.

Everest Calling

***Everest Calling* by Lorna Siggins**
ISBN 1 85188 663 6 192pp
United Kingdom: Mainstream Publishing; £14.99 (131) 5572959
United States: Traflagar Square Publishing, $34.95 (802) 457-1911

Chapter 10

by Lorna Siggins

> Day 42: refused planning permission for Camp Two, after a dodgy land decision. We proceed to further desecrate this sacred mountain by erecting Camp Three on the infamous North Coll (sic). Our extensive medical facilities are the toast of the mountain, and during our stay at Camp Three we are visited by a French climber with a broken leg and a Swede with broken English. We also perform a number of hip replacements on a group of visiting pensioners from Crumlin. Meanwhile, the summit beckons....
>
> Day 63: The treacherous North Col, perhaps the most hazardous of all mountain terrains, has often been compared to St. Patrick's Hill in cork on a frosty morning.....

The *Phoenix,* Ireland's equivalent of *Private Eye,* was clearly enjoying the Irish Everest expedition coverage. It was bait also for other wits at home. One sketch drew on the film *Alive,* the story of the Andean plane crash which was showing in cinemas at the time—the poor climbers had been hit by food shortages, and had been forced to eat *The Irish Times* reporter.

It was copy also for a colleague's humorous column. 'More difficult than Everest, more dangerous than K2, more sublime than the Matterhorn,' Brendan Glacken wrote, relating the tale of Reginald, Timothy, Jonathan, Tarquin and Joe, who were sponsored by Safe Harbour Bonding, the Inner Feelings Foundation and Ovaltine to climb 'New Man Mountain'. Lucky them: they were backed up by a team of 30 powerfully built female Sherpas—'without whom,' the author wrote, 'our equipment, never mind our consciousness, could never have been raised.'

On radio, Leslie Lawrence and Dermot Somers had become the voices of the expedition. The response from schools was overwhelming, and RTE's Pat Kenny transmitted regular messages of goodwill. Kenny was particularly taken by the fifth class of Our Lady of Victories Primary School in the north Dublin suburb of Ballymun. Under the supervision of their teacher, Brian O'Reilly, the boys had built an eight-foot model of Everest out of wood, chicken wire and newspaper. They had painted it and marked out the camps and the route. Later on, they held a base camp dinner in class in solidarity with the climbers. The menu was lukewarm tea, tuna chunks, pineapple, chapatis and yaktail soup.

The pressure on the team to succeed was mounting. The newspapers, radio stations, schools had their dates for the 'weather window' in early May. Within the first few days of the month, there were reports of multiple successes from the Nepalese side—37 people within 24 hours on 10 May. Frank Nugent had grabbed my arm up at Advance Base. Most of the climbers were huddled up there at 6,450 metres while the North Ridge reeled under the impact of bad weather. It must have been like a beach on the south side, to judge by the reports.

'What do you think they'll be saying back home?' he whispered.

There was one simple message that I had to put across in almost every report I sent—location, location, location; yes, the Irish expedition is on the ***North*** side of Everest! In any other year, there might not have been so much difficulty. However, this was the 40th anniversary of the Hillary- Tenzing climb, and British newspapers were full of reports about the large number of anniversary expeditions, and the environmental degradation on the Nepalese side. It was partly to avoid the south side squalor and relative lack of adventure that the Irish climbers had chosen the dark side of the mountain.

There was substance to the environmental concern. A global report on the state of the world's mountains, published the previous year was not the first to describe the route to Everest base camp in Nepal as decorated with the litter of many nations. Mountains were under severe pressure from such influences as migration, mining, hydroelectric schemes, tourism and climate change, it said. It identified the root cause as poverty, however. It argued that such environments require a high-altitude version of the sustainable development policies gaining ground throughout the developing world.

The expeditions commission of the regulatory international mountaineering body, Union Internationale des Associations d'Alpinisme (UIAA), had already issued regulations on rubbish removal. However, it was worried about the reaction of the Nepalese government which had decided to increase the peak fee on its side of the mountain from 10,000 to 50,000 US dollars and to impose a limit of one expedition per season on each of the three routes to the summit from Nepal.

The UIAA's expedition commission—of which Joss Lynam had been elected president—felt that this was a mistake. Unless it was complemented by restrictions on trekking in the area, it would hardly touch the pollution problem, and only international or commercial 'heavy duty' expeditions would be able to afford the fee.

Inevitably, the pre-monsoon season of 1993 would be an exception. All sorts of commemorative events were planned. The Royal Geographical Society had booked Lord Hunt, Hillary and other members of the Mount Everest foundation for an anniversary lecture in London on 26 May. Its monthly magazine *Geographical*, was billed as 'Everest anniversary special'; one advertisement placed by a Scottish distillery offered a limited edition 'Everest 40' blended whisky with some of its own single Highland malt dating back to 1953. A BBC film had George Lowe of the Hunt venture voicing the fear that Everest was becoming the 'greasy pole of Asia'. The romance had died long ago, Jan Morris, the reporter on the Hunt expedition, argued in *The Times*. Queen Elizabeth's coronation in June 1953 had been 'given fire' by the message from the mountain far away. Now, the monarchy was devalued, hundreds had climbed the highest summit.

'Fainter each year are the romantic images of Irvine and Mallory, lost in the mists.' All the more reason for choosing the challenge of the North side...

This sort of publicity was far more likely to affect the 21 expeditions at base camp on the Nepalese side; but it was small consolation when it was obvious that they were experiencing better weather. There was particular interest in the heavily financed British venture sponsored by DHL couriers, which included Rebecca Stephens, described as a *Financial Times* journalist, who was attempting to be the first British woman on the summit by the South Col. The leader was John Barry, a veteran climber with Northern Irish roots.

It was a little like living in an envelope after the trekkers had left. There was a sense of abandonment as the last of the Land Rovers disappeared in a whirl of dust, bound for Lhasa and sightseeing and a flight over Everest to Kathmandu, and, sadly, taking Rory McKee with them. A skilled and experienced mountaineer, he had not recovered from altitude sickness.

I had brought as many books as I could carry, and even a copy of the Morse code for studying at night by the light of a stout white candle brought in Kathmandu. Passing time was not a problem, though; the Base Camp library was good, the conversation was excellent, and there was always a laptop computer battery to be charged by generator, and copy to write.

After I came down from Advance Base, the newspaper was anxious to receive materials every day. Fresh snow was still falling, conditions were too unsettled to move. What could I write? There was much sympathy among the climbers—unaware, perhaps, of my reputation in the newsrooms for writing weather stories. Every morning I walked down the moraine and studied the mountain.

It began to take on a life. I learned to recognize its weather moods. The summit plume—spindrift in high winds—provided some diversion on clear days when there seemed to be nothing else to identify. It couldn't match the distinctive Irish cloudscape, however; and there were times when I yearn for a glimpse of the sea.

'Dawson just make sure you get up the bloody mountain when we get Camp Three in, okay?'

'Tony, just make sure you get Camp Three in, okay?'

The banter over the radio on the morning of Saturday, 15 May, was a change from the subdued tones of the previous week when wind was high and morale was low. On 14 May, the weather forecast from Bracknell indicated some clearance with winds abating over the next 48 hours. Four climbers, three Nepalese and John Maori and cameras left for the North Col; Maori had recruited the sturdy Jangbu as a technical assistant. The shift was like 'an explosion out of the camp'. Frank Nugent had said on the radio.

Dawson had outlined the plan to Leslie. There had been

continuing discussion at Advance Base after the meeting of 5 May, when it had been agreed that there would be two summit attempts by two groups of four. Now four climbers would move up from North Col to Camp Two—Robbie and Mick, who would carry gear accompanied by Tony, Richard, Khunke and Dendi. The following day, Tony and Richard would attempt to establish Camp Three, allowing Dawson and Frank to move up there unladen. The leader and his deputy had been selected as the first summit pair.

Dermot Somers was sick. Dr. Kathy Fleming, who had spent the last few days up at Camp Colgate, had diagnosed a possible blood clot in his leg, and he had suspected pleurisy. He would have to rest. Somers sounded philosophical about it on the radio. He had no intention of descending: he was no invalid.

Some 12 miles and over a thousand metres below at Base Camp, the optimism was infectious. John Bourke had arrived down from the second camp and so there was lively chat over dinner. Pulling his earlobe and waving his finger, Asha Rai had been talking to Khunke and Dendi on the radio. 'Around 17th, 18th, they will go for the summit, yes.'

It's incredibly slow, very dispiriting...I'm just on the 8,000 metre contour and I'm absolutely buggered.' The hoarse, gasping, Anglo-Irish tones over the radio were unmistakable. Richard O'Neil-Dean should have sounded more cheerful. This was to have been *his* day.

And that of Tony Burke. The paid had been due to make the carry to Camp Three, without oxygen. The forecast was for relatively gentle 15 to 20 knot winds, and both seemed in good shape. Burke had sustained slight frostnip on one hand, but he was the only member of the expedition at that stage to have spent two consecutive nights at 7,600 metres (25,000 feet).

They had set their alarm for 6 a.m., but had slept fitfully in the tent, secured with ropes to the mountainside. It was a 'howling' night; the fabric was hammered like a mainsail head to wind. Come the morning radio call, arranged for 9 a.m., they reported that they were ready to move but that it was too windy. Richard had almost set the tent on fire during the brew-up, and Tony had collapsed in a fit of uncontrollable giggles.

They waited, aware that they were losing valuable time. Responding from Advance Base, Dawson tried to reassure them. The Chinese had described the terrain between the second and third camps as the most exposed. 'It might ease further up.'

At 10 a.m., Khunke and Dendi decided to risk it, and it took Richard and Tony an hour to crawl out of the tent after them, each carrying about 12 kilos of basic gear and food. They were not on oxygen. It would be the last time that anyone would move beyond Camp Two without some oxygen feed.

The sky was clear, but the vexed zephyrs showed no signs of relenting. Mindful of Dawson's comments, they picked their way slowly, clambering over steep broken ground towards an abandoned Chinese camp just 100 metres above. It was to take them a full hour to complete that short journey, pulling on scraps of rope, scrambling around and about boulders and broken rock through the ice and snow.

It was, Richard recalled later, 'crushingly slow'. The ridge marked by towering cliffs was undefined. There was no obvious route ahead, and there were no fixed ropes above the first 50 metres. Despite the wind and the cold, he felt optimistic. He was well insulated and armed with a particularly heavy set of gloves.

His partner was not so happy. Tony Burke indicated that he was in trouble. The three layers of thermal gloves he was wearing did not seem to be sufficient cover for his frostnip. He could see the weather closing in, and had begun to think about his fingers. The tissue was already damaged. Was it worth losing a few digits and jeopardizing his career?

He signalled to Richard that he was going to leave his load at the Chinese camp and turn back. It was a psychological blow for both. It looked as if they would not now be able to complete the carry. O'Neil-Dean put in a radio call from the "peripatetic Camp Two'. It was not quite as exposed as where they had spent the night, he told Somers at Advance Base.

But the daysack felt incredibly heavy—'swinging out of your shoulders like a big gorilla', as Robbie Fenlon had described it before. Richard's description was more restrained: 'By the way,' the voice said cheerfully. 'Climbed your mountain yet?'

Richard decided that he would continue upward for another four to five hours. He had the radio. The wind was unrelenting, murky cloud was moving in, and it started to snow. He wasn't too worried about the welfare of Khunke and Dendi, because he was well aware of their experience. However, he was concerned that they might have turned round, passing him blind in the swirling spindrift, separated by troughs of soft snow.

Dermot Somers was on the radio watch at Advance Base, his bad leg stretched out on a stool. Progress was 'murderously slow, very dispiriting', Richard told him.

'You're well able for it,' Dermot responded. Had he been well enough, he would have liked to have done this carry himself. 'You sound very rational, very balanced, in control.'

'That's sage advice,' Richard replied. 'I'll keep going until five o'clock. And Dermot....it would have given me the utmost pleasure to have you here with me.'

He met the two Sherpas within the hour, shortly after he had broken out onto a steep snowfield, bordered by a sharp drop to the east. By then, the conditions had worsened considerably. Angry winds drove hail like a sandblast against his face. His head, his beard, his eyebrows were caked in ice. The slope was so open, so diffuse. With every step, the altitude sapped his strength.

Together, the three men considered their position. There was little daylight left, and Khunke estimated that it would take Richard another three hours to make it to 8,300 metres. He had left a load up there, he thought, while Dendi had stopped about 100 metres short. Richard did not relish the thought of being alone on the mountain with no established camp to shelter in above.

He was relieved to have met them, and he was wiped out. He dipped his rucksack with a karabiner to a scrap of fixed rope protruding from the snow. Someone would find it later and complete the journey to the top camp. For the first time, as he saw the two Nepalese disappearing below, he realized that he was beginning to feel quite cold. His six-foot-eight frame also felt the full force of the drumming wind. As he came off the rock and onto a wider area of shale, he recalled later that it must have been akin to 'trying to walk along an aeroplane wing while in flight'. He feared that he could be blown off the ridge and down into the East Rongburk glacier. Crouching, crawling, squatting, sliding, he eventually reached Camp Two.

His tent had been battered by the elements. As he ate some plum cake and tried to tidy up the contents, Dendi emerged. He was absolutely spun out. O'Neill-Dean persuaded the Sherpa to carry on with him, down to the North Col.

They made it in a state of near collapse, fighting the storm. It was impossible to stand. Their only option was to allow their weight to be supported laterally by the fixed ropes - 'a sort of Tyrolean traverse across the face of the mountain'. Dendi was having trouble with his eyes. Every 20 yards or so, they sank down into the snow, making it to the camp in the last of the evening light.

Richard met Dawson and Frank coming up the Col the following day. He could not hide his devastation. By the time he reached Advance Base, he was distraught. Stumbling over his words, he broke down and cried, inconsolably. 'That's what Himalayan climbing offers - extremes of sorrow and of triumph,' he said later, when he expressed regret at not having spent a little longer up on the mountain.

'The thing that just blew me away was how incredibly slow I was. I found that I was making progress of about 200 metres per hour over the ground. In retrospect, I'm sorry I didn't take one of Tony's oxygen bottles and a mask and put in on at the Chinese camp. I'd probably have done much better, at the cost of using some oxygen at the height on the mountain. It would have meant that my load would have been higher for Dawson and Frank. Every extra hour up there would have been worth it. I can say that now, but then there seemed to be no other decision to take. Yet I had such a crushing sense of disappointment afterwards that it took me some time to deal with that.'

The idea that he might have broken the 8,000 metre contour for the first time in Irish climbing and almost completed the most difficult leg on the summit approach was of little consolation to him. He didn't have his altimeter with him, so the new record in Irish mountaineering could not be confirmed until his rucksack was located. But he had 'tasted' the approach to the summit. 'And it felt quite climbable...'

Gao, our interpreter, was to bring us the news at Base Camp from the other side of the mountain. He had heard on the radio that another 17 people had reached the summit from the Nepalese side.

Yesterday it blew stink around the snout of the Rongbuk glacier at 17,000 feet - stink and bin lids, prayer flags, stones and pebbles, even an emergency toilet tent. For once, the scavenging yellow-billed choughs fought shy of the lean-to kitchen where the Nepalese cook, Aka Raj, baked brown bread in charcoal. Only a lone rose finch clung valiantly to a nearby rock.

As for the dust, it was ubiquitous: in eyes, hair, up sleeves, down socks, on cups, plates, in dinner and tea. As it is, food supplies at Base Camp are beginning to run low. Four climbers who came down to recuperate almost turned back when they heard about the diet of tinned tuna and spam. They've stayed, for now...

Well, even an occasional rockfall from the moraine above Base Camp was worth writing about now. Confidence in the forecasts from Bracknell had been shaken. I had taken on a Pepsy mantle, having been assigned the task of log and weather forecast recorder. I never liked being the bearer of bad news. But now it was warning of high winds and unsettled conditions. Stelfox, Nugent and Mike Barry, who had agreed to support them on their summit bid, retreated to Advance Base with Hangbu and John Maori. They would have to defer their plans.

Or abandon them altogether? No one talked of failure yet, but the days were slipping by. On 18 May, day 63, John Bourke hired the Swiss jeep and went with heavy heart and Gao and Lawang to Passurn to order the yaks for departure. The previous day, he and Lawrence had taught the Chinese pair a little Irish; they had also cleaned the Chinese toilet.

Bourke arrived back to find climbers at Base Camp. Richard, Tony and Rabbi were down. Within 24 hours, Dermot and Dr. Kathy Fleming had also arrived. She was obviously worried about her patient. He had resisted their attempts to have him carried down in case the suspected blood clot went to his heart or lungs with fatal consequences. He walked down instead. Hood up to shield his ravaged features from the wind, he was wraith-like. He doubled up every so often, breaking into a cavernous cough.

So this was what Tibet did to you, he observed a couple of nights later after dinner in the mess tent. Nepal imbued warmth and ease, but the very quality that drew one to Tibet - the stark, spare, harsh and arid landscape - left one a dried out husk. It was as if life itself was suspended, as if nothing could survive. Even the North Col was like a 'frozen wave'.

Vertical pleasure

Vertical Pleasure: The Secret Life of a Taxman **by Mick Fowler**
EXCERPT FROM (PAGE 101)—THE GOLDEN PILLAR OF SPANTIK
ISBN 0 340 623217 £17.99 223pp
United Kingdom: Hodder & Stoughton Publishers; (1171) 8736000
United States: Cloudcap Publishing: (206) 365-9192

The Golden Pillar of Spantik
by Mick Fowler

Feeling rather unsettled I returned to the climbing. Above me the short slope eased as I gained the right bounding edge of the pillar. Across to my right monstrous ice cliffs overhanging awe-inspiring avalanche-ridden gullies seemed surprisingly close, whilst further right again was our proposed line of descent: a snow and ice spur of a modest angle low down but increasing to a steep-looking ice slope in its upper section. A surrounding fringe of cornices looked potentially exciting at the top but worries in that direction were a long way off yet. Also evident from our view point was the fact that the summit snowfields were anything but straightforward–it would be challenging enough just reaching the flat area above the descent ridge. All in all it was not really very encouraging from the point of view of the descent; we had been aware of potential difficulties when studying the ground through binoculars but from close quarters it seemed more problematical than expected. It was still preferable to descending the spur, which often seemed to lack good belay points and the lower slopes of which we knew became dangerously avalanche-prone in bad weather.

Turning back to the problem in hand, we had reached an area of snowy ledges leading up to a hard-looking powder-blasted corner above which our proposed line was out of sight. We had also just moved out of the extreme cold of the shade and into the enervating heat of the sun. Progress withered to a halt. Although the sun was out it was obvious that we were in for a period of snow. Huge grey clouds were racing across towards us and no further incentive was needed to pitch the tent as soon as possible.

A third of the floor area hung over thin air but the other two thirds gave reasonably flat sleeping quarters, and as long as we avoided the lighter area of groundsheet, all would be well.

Soon the familiar sound of snow drumming on tent fabric brought back nasty memories. I engrossed myself in *Gorky Park* whilst Victor busied himself with the continuous brewing technique, struggling to melt vast quantities of powder snow. Most commendable, I thought.

'Lazy bastard,' said Victor.

Fifteen hours later–at 6 a.m. the following morning–it was still snowing heavily and fifty centimetres of new powder threatened to nudge the tent from the ledge. Nevertheless the ground ahead did not seem to be avalanche-prone and after an initial dither we decided to press on. Route-finding would be a problem if the bad weather persisted but at least we had seen the first 100 metres the afternoon before and so knew where to start. A sixty-degree snow slope leading to the powder-blasted corner looked easy but proved to be ten-centimetre deep powder lying on smooth slabs. It gave climbing at least as difficult as the vertical corner which followed although that consisted of ninety-degree brittle ice and required continuous clipping into the ice-axes, not to mention the masochism involved in clearing fifteen centimetres of powder from the ice.

By midday things were looking better; we had managed 200 metres and the weather was clearing again. A fine ledge (the only one on the entire pillar) provided a welcome stopping point and, as Victor pointed out to me, an ideal opportunity to do all the things that ledges or flat ground allow one to do in comfort. Unfortunately it was too early for us to justify spending the night here.

From Base Camp the binoculars had shown that the next section consisted of very steep rock walls with a series of parallel snowbands running diagonally from left to right. All but one of the bands had appeared to lead to rock walls set at an extremely high angle which, when considered in the context of the temperature extremes and altitude, could well present insuperable problems. It was therefore vital that we chose the right line.

From our vantage point on the platform we peered hopefully upwards. The strata of the rock was such that numerous left-to-right slanting grooves ran up an overhanging rock wall for about thirty metres to where the angle eased and we knew the snowbands began. With me taking the easiest option by tackling the shortest groove, Victor was treated to the entertaining spectacle of me demonstrating my incompetence at aid climbing. The hail of lighthearted abuse was difficult to deny but the end result was effective and we gained the base of a snowy ramp. The bad weather was back with us by now but at least we seemed to have chosen the right line. Easier ground with only short hard steps, led up into the driving snow until we found ourselves in a steep and horrifyingly constricted chimney–an exhausting pitch which fortunately was Victor's lead. It was now well past our usual bivi time but absolutely nothing suitable was in sight. The last thing I wanted to do was climb on into the biting cold of the night. But what could we do?

More very hard climbing led to a horizontal band of ice; it was getting dark by now and, despite initial opposition from Victor, I insisted that we should spend the night here. In the rush to get ourselves established I managed to pull the wires from the back of my head torch and consequently enjoyed intermittent periods of unwanted darkness for the rest of the route.

It quickly became apparent that things were not going as planned. Wherever we started cutting, the ice turned out to be only about five centimetres thick–we couldn't even place a decent ice-screw, let alone cut a satisfactory bum ledge. Victor went unusually quiet and I cursed and swore–very much aware of who had insisted on stopping here.

One ten-centimetre diameter stone projected from the slope and two hours of effort punctuated by numerous tangles (and fumbles in the dark from me) saw us 'sitting' on a ten-centimetre-wide 'ledge' both struggling to get our feet on the solitary stone. Victor decided to tie his rucksack in to the belay and spend the night standing in it whilst I opted for relying more on the support given by my harness. Both of us were suspended from the same jammed nut, whilst tied-off ice-screws held the ten/bivi bag in position. Equipment fell to the bottom of the tent fabric pulling it tight and smothering our faces. Something told me that it was not going to be a pleasant night.

'As bad as being sat in the Tax Office?' quipped Victor, keen as ever to bring my employers into the conversation.

'No. Worse.' My answer required no hesitation. 'Squeezed next to you all night–awful prospect.'

'Likewise,' came from somewhere in the dark next to me.

There is nothing like a bit of feeble abuse to keep the spirits up.

The onset of snow was almost the last straw; it was not so much that it snowed heavily but the expanse of face above caused waves of spindrift to engulf us at regular intervals. The valance around the tent entrance proved to be a perfect receptacle for this and it soon piled up on top of the entrance zip, effectively blocking our only means of escape. Every now and then one of us would uncontrollably scream obscenities–unable to suffer the claustrophobia a moment longer–rip open the zip for a breath of fresh air and suffer a face full of powder snow, some of which inevitably found its way deep into the warmth of our sleeping bags.

Suffice to say that the night was long and miserable, although fortunately the weather turned out to be better than it had sounded; our spindrift problems were caused chiefly by shifting snow higher on the mountain, rather than actual precipitation.

The dry cold air and heavy breathing was by now irritating our throats. Both of us had niggling coughs and for me there was a definite sensation of something stuck in my throat. During the night I made several disgusting attempts to cough up this blockage, and when I managed to, just as we prepared to leave the bivi, a strip of flesh appeared, perhaps one centimetre long and half a centimetre wide. I stared aghast at what I had done. There was an awful hiatus as I wondered whether I would be able to speak properly and how much pain there would be in swallowing. Tentatively rediscovering the qualities of my throat and larynx, it was with more than a slight feeling of relief that I found everything seemed to function normally. There still seemed to be a frog in my throat but there was no way that I would be making any effort to clear it further.

This aside, the morning's preparation was a nightmare of cold fingers, wooden toes and assorted tangles–it was truly a pleasure to be on the move again. Day six from Base Camp started with a couple of standard insecure pitches taking us to the start of the final snow ramp which could now be seen to lead to a fortuitous gap between the top of the pillar and the seracs, which were draped from the summit icefields. A monstrous 100-metre high ear-shaped sérac was visible overhanging the gap through which we would have to climb. The ramp was about two metres wide and continually hard–one pitch in particular being a nightmare of scraping crampons on seventy-degree rock, no runners and the prospect of a big, big fall down the vertical wall below as a penalty for any mistake. It was a fine nerve-wracking lead by Victor which led to a point directly beneath the exit gap and–less favourably–exactly in the line of fire of the giant ice ear (not to mention lots of associated smaller ears). The last hard pitch loomed above, an eighty-degree corner choked with powder, overlaying a veneer of ice. Both of us glanced anxiously at the thousands of tons of ice poised directly above. Careful movements were the order of the day–no hefty thumps on peg-runners here, more delicate taps and gentle clips into deftly inserted axe placements. It was a hard pitch, both mentally and physically, but the end was in sight–above it only fifty metres of snow slope remained. Somehow Victor found the energy to produce the necessary waist-deep trench and we were on the plateau at last. All technical difficulty lay behind us. I flopped limply on to horizontal ground; the immediate pleasure was a properly erected tent and somewhere flat to lie down. Any elation could wait till later.

In England I had confided in friends that I would be satisfied if we managed to climb the pillar but could not get to the summit. Now we were actually here, it seemed unthinkable that we should not try.

But success was far from a certainty. Morning revealed the top to be a depressingly long way off. We had originally planned to take all our equipment part way and collect it whilst heading down towards the 'descent spur'. Now, however, it seemed that progress would be challenging enough just with light sacks, so our tent and hardware were duly left behind.

Plodding limply in Victor's steps I had no doubt as to whether we had made the right decision. It was all I could do to keep going at all–our rate of progress was so painfully slow and the summit so distressingly distant it just seemed inconceivable that we would ever make it. With sufficient rests the pace could be maintained–the difficult part was keeping alive the will to continue when it seemed such an impossible task in the time available.

Cold was also becoming a real problem. The powdery snow at this altitude was making our feet uncomfortably cold. Hands were fine–if our fingers became cold we could quickly warm them down our trousers or under armpits. Feet, however, were logistically more difficult to warm in this manner. For me the best technique seemed to be to lift them out of the snow and (energy permitting) shake them vigorously in the air. This looked rather silly and didn't aid progress too well; it also prompted Victory to get the camera out a lot.

'Must send these shots to your boss,' he kept saying.

Inevitably the result was the foot-waving stops were kept to a minimum and cold feet were something we had to live with. Frostbite, though, is a deep concern of mine and I found the time when I had no feeling in my toes deeply disturbing.

The day developed into an endless masochistic trudge. Surrounded by magnificent views I could only stare blankly at the tracks and envelop myself in the exhaustion of every step. At best we sank in ankle deep–at worst genuinely waist deep and always in the penetrating cold of feathery powder snow. Victor was a tower of strength on this sort of ground. I found the lack of any firm footing and the constant struggle to stay upright totally enervating. Give me technical climbing any day.

It seemed incredible that the summit was getting closer but at 12:50 p.m. our efforts were rewarded–we could go up no more. At 7027 metres our goal was achieved, everything suddenly seemed worthwhile–from the masochism of the last six and a half hours to the bureaucratic hurdles of the last eighteen months.

We stayed for forty-five minutes waiting for the never-to-appear hole in the clouds before scurrying back to the tent, hotly pursued by crackling electricity and swirling spindrift. Now we had only to get down. A glimmer of elation grew in the depth of my heart.

Two long days later we had cautiously crossed crevasse minefields, abseiled from powder-snow mushrooms, lowered each other through cornices and very nearly been avalanched, but success was ours. The glimmer had developed into a hearty glow. Safe at last, we had completed the untrodden descent spur and could now wallow in the warmth of Base Camp and relish our cook's hugs and flower garlands.

It was Thursday evening–I had to be back at work on Monday morning. The journey was a little tiring but suffice it to say that on Monday the civil servant shoes were duly in position under the civil servant desk. My other life had begun again.

Geoffrey Winthrop Young

***Geoffrey Winthrop Young* by Alan Hankinson**
EXCERPT FROM (PAGE 123)—ALPINE FIRST ASCENTS
ISBN 0 340 57609 365pp
United Kingdom: Hodder & Stoughton, £18.99 (1171) 8736000

Alpine First Ascents

by Alan Hankinson

During the summer term he worked hard, but found time for a half-hearted flirtation: "Thought myself in love with Rachel Kaye Shuttleworth, but was glad when we settled not to pursue the subject. *Sic transit*! Anyway, more time etc. for a motor car, which at least can travel about with me." Then came the summer holidays and the Alps again and a better, busier season than ever.

He summed it up in the Journal: "Unique season–new climbs on Breithorn, Dom, Täschhorn, Weisshorn etc. Week at Montenvert; 21 hours on Requin by wrong route, two Drus, circuit of Grépon, Charmoz and Blaitères in one day. Täschhorn with Ryan, and did not expect for about six hours to get back alive. Had Knubel for the year."

They were all superb climbs but the outstanding one was the first ascent of the tremendous South face of the Täschhorn. The story has become one of the legends of alpine achievement–for the formidable nature of the route and also for the terrifying intensity of Geoffrey's account in *On High Hills*. He wrote it twenty years after the event, and it shows how vividly the details of the ordeal lodged in his memory–not only the nature of the terrain and the climbing and the weather but also the grim sensations that the climbers had to endure. The account, covering more than twenty printed pages, has a compelling, nightmarish quality, conveying–to my mind, more powerfully than any other passage of mountain writing–what it must feel like to be in a bad and dangerous place, in bad weather, fighting for apparently endless hours, always desperate and often close to despair, to force a way through. The man who led them through the crux section was Franz Lockmatter, and Geoffrey prefaced his description with a high tribute:

> Franz Lockmatter's mountaineering feat was the greatest I have witnessed, and after a number of years I can still say the greatest I can imagine. It is right that it should be recorded; for I do not suppose that in its mastery of natural difficulty, in its resistance to the effects of cold and fatigue and to the infections of depression and fear, it has often been equalled on any field of adventure or conflict.

The party was the same one that had climbed the Matterhorn and the Weisshorn the year before–Ryan with his two Lochmatter guides, Geoffrey with Knubel. The route was, indeed, the one that Ryan and Geoffrey had surveyed and discussed on their descent from the Weisshorn. Now they attempted it.

The weather was discouraging. After a night at the Täschalp hut, they set off before dawn in a cold drizzle which they withstood for a while before retreating "to a day of chess and wild-raspberry jam". They made an earlier start the next morning, in colder but clearer air, and raced up the snow slopes that led to the foot of the face. The western buttress above them was steep and liberally plastered with fresh snow, but the holds were plentiful enough to allow them to climb unroped–Ryan's party first, with him between the two guides; Geoffrey and Knubel following.

At 7:30 a.m. they paused on a rock ledge to eat a quick breakfast, standing up. It was their last food and their last rest for many hours. The open face above them was steeper, so they roped up at this point–Josef Lockmatter, Ryan, then Franz–then Geoffrey, with Knubel bringing up the rear. They climbed on, finding no stances where they might rest a moment and no rocky knobs where they could hitch the rope and get some sense of protection. After a long time a rope was tied between Franz Lockmatter and Geoffrey, so that all five men were now linked together, none of them with any doubts that a fall by one of them would most likely bring all of them crashing down. Fingers and feet were numbed by the intense cold. It was snowing again. All of them were worrying about the situation they were in, and even more about the situation they would be in if they found there was no way up above them.

They spotted a gully high above and to one side, and thought it might make for easier progress, so they made a delicate, ascending traverse to gain it. But when they reached it, one glance was enough to know that there was no route there. So Josef Lockmatter climbed carefully down to the bed of the gully and inspected the snow-spattered wall beyond.

"It won't go," he shouted up to them.

"But it *must* go," Franz shouted back, and set off down to join his brother and take over the lead. At this point in his narrative, Geoffrey contrasted the climbing styles of the brothers:

> Josef, and other great guides, on slabs moved with the free poise of an athlete and the foot-cling of a chamois. Franz, in such case, had the habit and something of the appearance of a spider or crustacean. His curled head disappeared altogether. His body and square shoulders split and elongated into four steely tentacles, radiating from a small central core or hub of intelligence, which transmitted the messages between his tiny hands and boots as they clung attached and writhing at phenomenal angles and distances.

They resumed climbing, with Franz leading and Knubel, now carrying all the rucksacks and ice axes, in the rear. The weather had grown danker. "The fight went on doggedly," Geoffrey wrote, "with that determination to take no long view but to make just the next hold good and the one more step secure, which enables a human atom to achieve such heights of effort and to disregard such lengths of suffering."

They found their way into a narrow chimney which afforded some sense of protection. Josef Lockmatter took the lead again and for a while the climbing was easier. Their hopes rose that the chimney might signal the end of their struggle:

And then, it all ended! The chimney simply petered out: not under the south-east ridge, as we might have hoped, but in the very hard heart of the diamond precipice some six hundred feet below the final and still invisible summit. The vague exit from the chimney faded out against the base of a blank cliff. One of its side walls led on for a little, and up to the left. There it too vanished, under the lower rim of a big snowy slab, sloping up, and slightly conical, like a dish-cover. I have reason to remember that slab. It formed the repellent floor of a lofty, triangular recess. On its left side, and in front, there was space and ourselves. On its right, and at the back, a smooth leap of colossal cliff towered up for a hundred feet of crystallized shadow, and then arched out above our heads in a curve like the dark underside of a cathedral dome. A more appalling-looking finish to our grim battle of ascent could hardly have been dreamed in a "falling" nightmare; and we had not even standing room to appreciate it worthily! As I looked up and then down, I had an overpowering sense of the great grey wings behind us, shadowing suddenly close across the whole breadth of precipice, and folding us off finally from the world.

But our long apprenticeship to discouragement stood us in good stead. Muscles braced anew obstinately; determination quickened resentfully. The recess on whose lip we hung had been formed by the sliding of a great wedge of rock off the inclined, dish-cover slab, once its bed. But on our right the cliff continued the original line. My impression of this, therefore, was as of a high building viewed from under one corner. Its sheer front wall stretched away to the right, flush with the sill of our slab. The end wall of the building formed the right side of our recess, and over-hung the slab. The rectangular house-corner, where the two walls joined, rose immediately above us, vertical and iced, but a little chipped by the rending out of the wedge. Again, the front wall of this projecting house did not rise to the same height as the cliff that backed our recess. Forty feet up–my measures are merely impressions–the wall slanted steeply back in a roof, receding out of sight. Presumably another huge wedge had here slid from its bed, on a higher plane. Above and beyond this roof the precipices rose again into sight, in the same line and of the same height as the cliffs which backed our recess. Only, the cliff vertically above us was crowned by the great dome or overhang. There must be, therefore, invisible above, some rough junction or flaw where the line of cliffs above the receding house-roof linked on to the forward jut of our dome. Four vital questions suggested themselves: Could the house-corner be climbed? Was the roof, if attainable, too steep to crawl up? Might there be a flawed connection where the precipice upon which the roof abutted joined on the side of the dome? If there was such a flaw, would this yield us a passage out on to the face of the convex dome *above* its circle of largest dimension, on its retreating upper curve, or *below* it, under its hopeless arch? These details are tiresome, perhaps unintelligible. But they may help other climbers to a better understanding of Franz's remarkable feat.

Right up in the angle of the recess there was a rotund blister of rock modelled in low relief on the face of the slab; and round this a man, hunched on small nicks in the steep surface, could just belay the rope. Josef and Franz were crouching at this blister up in the recess. The rest of us were dispersed over freezing cling-holds along the lower rim of the slab. And the debate proceeded, broken by gusts of snow. The man to lead had clearly to run out a hundred to a hundred and fifty feet of rope. He could be given no protection. His most doubtful link would come some eighty feet up, above the roof. If he found a flaw there and it served him favourable, he would be out on the convex of the dome fully a hundred feet above us, and outside us in a direct line above our heads. If, at this point, he could not proceed–well, it was equally unlikely that he could return!

Franz showed no hesitation. The hampered preparations for the attempt went on hurriedly. We had all to unrope as best we could, so as to arrange for the two hundred feet of possible run-out, and we hooked on to our holds with difficulty, while the snow-frozen rope kinked and banged venomously about us. In the end little J. and I had to remain off the rope, to leave enough free. Then– as a flame

Stirred by the air, under a cavern gaunt–

Franz started up the corner, climbing with extraordinary nerve but advancing almost imperceptibly. It was much like swarming up the angle of a tower, rough-cast with ice. Ryan and little J. crept up near the blister; but as there was no more room I remained hanging on to the fractured sill of the slab. In this position I was farther out; and I could just see Franz's two feet scratting desperately for hold to propel him up to the tilt of the roof above the corner. The rest of him was now out of sight. The minutes crawled like hours, and the rope hanging down to us over the gable-end hardly seemed to stir upwards. The snow gusts distracted us cruelly. A precipice in sunshine seems at least interested in our microscopic efforts. Its tranquillity even helps our movement by giving to it a conspicuous importance. But when the stable and the unstable forces of nature join in one of their ferocious, inconclusive conflicts, the little human struggle is carelessly swallowed up in uproar, and tosses unregarded and morally deflated, like a wet straw on a volcanic wave.

Suddenly I heard that unmistakable scrape and grit of sliding boot-nails and clothes. Above my head, over the edge of the roof to the right. I saw Franz's legs shoot out into space. Time stopped. A shiver, like expectancy, trembled across the feeling of unseen grey wings behind me, from end to end of the cliff. I realized impassively that the swirl of the rope must sweep me from my holds before it tightened on the doubtful belay of the blister. But fate was playing out the game in regions curiously remote. My mind watched the moves, itself absorbed into the same remote, dispassionate atmosphere. It seemed unwilling to disturb the issue by formulating a thought, or even a fear. The fact of the body seemed negligible; it had no part in the observant aloofness into which all consciousness had withdrawn. Something of the same feeling of separation between the body and the watching mind is the experience of men actually falling or drowning, when action is at an end and there is not even pain to reunite bodily and mental sensation. But during the crises of this day the condition lasted, with me certainly, for spaces that could only be measured by hours.

Franz's boots again disappeared above the edge. No one in the recess had known of the slip, out of their sight and lost in the gusts. He had stopped himself miraculously on the rim by crushing his hands on to ice-dimples in the slab. The hanging rope began again to travel up along the slanting gable-end of the roof. There was a long interval and now and then the sound of a scratting boot, or the scrabble of loose surface. Then the rope began, jerkily, to work out and across far above our heads. Franz had found a flaw in the join of the cliffs above the roof, and he was creeping out on to the projection of the dome. The lengthening rope now hung down well *outside* the men in the recess, and it might have hung outside me on the lower rim, had they not held in its end. Its weight upon Franz, as it swayed down through the snow, must have added to his immense difficulties. He was well out of sight, clinging somewhere above on the upper curve of the overhang.

An indistinct exchange of shouts began, half swallowed by echo, wind, and snow. Franz, it appeared was still quite uncertain if he could get up any further. For the time he could hold on well enough to help one man with the rope; but he had not two hands free to pull. I could hear his little spurt of laughter at the question–"Could he return?" He suggested that Josef should join him, and the rest wait until they two might return with a rescue-party. Wait, there!–for at best fifteen hours hanging on to the icy holds, in a snow wind! Well, then, what if we four tried to get down, and he would go on alone–if he could? "Get down? Ho, la, la!"–Josef was at his resourceful wits' end. I suggested pacifyingly, that Ryan might join and reinforce Franz, and that we remaining three could attempt the descent together. This provoked the crisis, which had been long threatening. Josef's competence and control were second to none in the Alps; but the responsibility, the physical strain, and this last disappointment had overstrained the cord. it snapped; and in somewhat disconcerting fashion.

Harsh experience can teach us that when these accidiæ occur, as they may to the most courageous of men if tested unfairly, the only remedy is to soothe or to startle. The first was impracticable in our situation. I spoke sharply in reproach, but without raising my voice. The experiment succeeded surprisingly. Self-control returned upon the instant, and for the rest of the day Josef climbed and safeguarded us with all his own superb skill and chivalrous consideration.

He was right in so far that, at that hour of the day and upon those treacherous cliffs, now doubly dangerous under accumulating snow, all odds were against any of us who turned back getting down alive. Franz in any case could not get back to us, and he might not be able to advance. We were committed, therefore, to the attempt to join him, however gloomy its outlook. As many as possible must be got up to him–and the rest must be left to chance.

Josef started his attempts on the corner. This left room for me to move up to Ryan on the slab. He asked me, I remember, what I thought were the chances of our escape. I remember, too, considering it seriously, and I can hear myself answering–"About one in five." As we talked fragmentarily, and listened to the distant scraping of Josef's feet up the roof, I recalled–with a grim appreciation of this new, first-hand example–having often remarked in the stories of shipwreck or other catastrophe how inevitably and usefully the "educated" man plays up to the occasion. For the audience of his own mind as much as for anybody else he sustains almost unconsciously the part which his training imposes upon him as alone consistent with his self-respect.

The end of the long rope hooted down past us. It hung outside the recess, dangling in air; and I could only recover it by climbing down again over the rim of the slab and reaching out for it one-handed with my axe. I passed it up; and then I stayed there, hanging on, because I could no longer trust hands or feet to get me up the slope again. Ryan began the corner; but if I have described the position at all intelligibly, it will be seen that while the corner rose vertically on our right, the long rope hung down on a parallel line from the dome directly above our heads. So it came that the higher we climbed up the corner the more horizontal became the slanting pull of the rope, and the more it tended to drag us sideways off the corner and back under the overhang. Very coolly, Ryan shouted a warning before he started of the insufficient power left in frozen hands. Some twenty feet up, the rope tore him from his inadequate, snowy holds. He swung across above our heads and hung suspended in mid-air. The rope was fixed round his chest. In a minute it began to suffocate him. He shouted once or twice to the men above to hurry. Then a fainter call, "I'm done," and he dangled to all appearance unconscious on the rope. Franz and Josef could only lift him half-inch by half-inch. For all this hour–probably it was longer–they were clamped one above the other on to the steep face of the dome, their feet on shallow but sound nicks, one hand clinging on, and only the other free to pull in. Any inch the one lifted, the other held. The rough curve of the rock, over which the higher portion of the rope descended, diminished by friction the effectiveness of each tug. The more one considers their situation, the more superhuman do the co-operation and power of two men displayed during this time, at the end of all those hours of effort, appear. Little J. and I had only the deadly anxiety of watching helplessly, staring upward into the dizzy snow and shadow: and that was enough. J. had followed silently and unselfishly the whole day; and even now he said nothing: crouching in unquestioning endurance beside the freezing blister on the slab.

Ryan was up at last, somehow, to the overhang; and being dragged up the rough curve above. A few small splinters were loosened, and fell, piping, past me and on to me. I remember calculating apathetically whether it was a greater risk to try and climb up again into the recess, unroped and without any feel in fingers and toes, or to stay where I was, hanging on to the sill, and chance being knocked off by a stone. It is significant of the condition of body and mind that I decided to stay where I was, where at least stiffened muscles and joints still availed to hold me mechanically fixed on to my group of rounded nicks.

Ryan was now out of sight and with the others. When the constriction of the rope was removed he must have recovered amazingly toughly, and at once; for down once more, after a short but anxious pause, whistled the snow-stiffened rope, so narrowly missing me that little J. cried out in alarm. I could not for a time hook it in with the axe; and while I stretched, frigidly and nervously, Josef hailed me from seemingly infinite height, his shouts travelling out on the snow eddies. They could not *possibly* pull up my greater weight. Unless I felt sure I could stick on to the corner and manage to climb round to them by Franz's route, it was useless my trying! At last I had fished in the rope, with a thrill of relief, and I set mental teeth. With those two tied onto the rope above, and myself tied on–in the way I meant to tie myself onto the rope below, there were going to be no more single options. We were all in it together; and if I had still some faith in myself I had yet more in that margin of desperation strength which extends the possible indefinitely for such men as I knew to be linked on to me above. And if I were once up, well there would be no question after that about little J. coming up too!

I gave hands and feet a last blue-beating against the rock to restore some feeling to them. Then I knotted the rope round my chest, made the loose end into a triple-bowline "chair" round the thighs, and began scratching rather futilely up the icy rectangular corner. For the first twenty-five feet–or was it much less?–I could just force upward. Then the rope began to drag me off inexorably. I clutched furiously up a few feet more; and then I felt I must let go, the drag was too strong for frozen fingers. As I had already resolved, at the last second I kicked off from the rock with all my strength. This sent me flying out on the rope, and across under the overhang, as if attached to a crazy pendulum. I could see J. crouching in the recess far below, instinctively protecting his head. The impetus jumped the upper part of the rope off its cling to the rock face of the dome above, and enabled the men to snatch in a foot or two. The return-swing brought me back, as I had half hope, against the corner, a little higher up. I gripped it with fingers and teeth, and scrambled up another few feet. But the draw was now irresistible. I kicked off again; gained a foot or so, and spun back.

I was now up the corner proper, I should have been by rights scrambling up the roof on the far side of my gable edge. But the rope if nothing else, prevented any chance of my forcing myself over it and farther to the right. Another cling and scratch up the gable end, and I was not far below the level of the dome overhanging above and to my left. For the last time I fell off. This time the free length of the rope, below its hold upon the curve of the dome, was too short to allow of any return swing. So I shot out passively, to hang, revolving slowly, under the dome, with the feeling that my part was at an end. When I spun around inward, I looked up at the reddish, scarred wall freckled with snow, and at the tense rope, looking thin as a grey cobweb and disappearing frailly over the forespring of rock that arched greedily over my head. When I spun outward, I looked down–no matter how many thousand feet–to the dim, shifting lines of the glacier at the foot of the peak, hazy through the snowfall; and I could see, well inside my feet, upon the dark face of the precipice the little blanched triangle of the recess and the duller white dot of J.'s face as he crouched by the blister. It flashed across me, absurdly, that he ought to be more anxious about the effect of my gymnastics upon the fragile thread of alpine rope, his one link with hope, than about me!

I was quite comfortable in the chair, but the spinning had to be stopped. I reached out the axe at full stretch, and succeeded in touching the cliff, back under the overhang. This stopped me, face inward. I heard inarticulate shouting above, and guessed its meaning, although I was now too close under the dome to catch the words:–"They could not lift my dead weight!" I bethought me, and stretched out the axe again; got its point against a wrinkle of the wall, and pushed out. This started me swinging straight out and in below the dome. After two pokes I swung in near enough to be able to give a violent, short-armed thrust against the cliff. It carried me out far enough to jump quite a number of feet of rope clear of its cling down the rock above. The guides took advantage of the easing to haul in, and I pendulum'd back a good foot higher. The cliff facing me was now beginning to spring out in the Gothic arch of the overhang; so it could be reached more easily. I repeated the shove-out more desperately. Again they hauled in on the released rope. This time I came back close under the arch; and choosing a spot as I swung in, I lifted both feet, struck them at the wall and gave a convulsive upward and outward spring. The rope shortened up; and as I banged back the cornice of the arch loomed very near above my head. But the free length of rope below it was now too short to let me again reach to the back of the arch with leg or axe. I hung, trying in vain to touch the lowest moulding of the cornice above with my hands. I heard gasps and grunts above quite distinctly now. The rope strained and creaked, gritting over the edge of the rock above me. I felt the tremor of the sinews heaving on it. But for all that, I did not move up. I reached up with the axe in both hands, just hooked the pick into a lucky chink of the under-moulding, and pulled, with a frantic wriggle of the whole body. It was a feeble lift, but enough for the sons of Anak above to convert into a valuable gain. The axe slipped down on to my shoulder, held there by its sling. I reached up and back with both arms, got hold of a finger-grip and gained another inch. Infinitesimal inches they seemed, each a supreme effort, until my nose and chin scratched up against a fillet of the cornice. Then the arms gave out completely, so much at the end of their strength that they dropped lifeless. But the teeth of the upper jaw held on a broken spillikin and with the stronger succour of the rope, supported me for the seconds while the blood was running back into my arms.

Wrestle by wrestle it went on. Every reserve of force seemed exhausted by the impulse was now supplied by a flicker of hope. Until, at last, I felt my knee catch over a moulding on the edge, and I could sink forward for an instant's rest, with rucked clothes clinging over the rough, steep, upward but *backward* curving of the dome. It is impossible to suggest the relief of that feeling, the proof

> that the only solid surface which still kept me in touch with existence had ceased to thrust itself out for ever as a barrier overhead, and was actually giving back below me in semi-support.
>
> But there was no time, or inclination, to indulge panting humanity with a rest or a realization. I crept up a few feet, on to small, brittle, but sufficient crinkles. The dark figures of the three men above were visible now, clinging crab-like and exhausted on to similar nicks, indistinct in the snow dusk, but still human company.

The climb was still far from over. It was snowing more heavily now and there was a long wait while they got the rope down to Knubel and he struggled up, laden as he was, to join them. All were exhausted, unsure that they would find a way out but absolutely certain that they could never go back the way they had ascended.

Geoffrey's account devotes more than a page to his thoughts during the experience, the way in which his initial fears evaporated rapidly to be replaced by "the feeling of belonging to an impersonal, timeless existence".

It was late afternoon and the fight went on: "I can recall nothing but obscurity, steepness, and an endless driving of the muscles to their task. Still no message of hope reached us from above; and yet we must have left another 400 feet of rib and crack, snow-ice and equivocal holds below us. Even fancy dared not whisper to itself of the summit: the next five feet, and still the next five feet were the end of all effort and expectation."

At last the angle of the slope began to ease and suddenly Geoffrey found himself on summit ridge, close to the top. He halted there to protect Knubel's ascent, then the two of them trudged up to join the others: "We found them, relaxed in spent attitudes on the summit-slabs, swallowing sardines and snow, our first food since half past seven in the morning. It was now close upon six o'clock. Franz came across to meet me, and we shook hands. 'You will never do anything harder than that, Franz!' 'No,' he said reflectively, 'man could not do much more.'"

Banff Mountain Book Festival

The Banff Mountain Book Festival is a celebration of mountain literature which brings together writers, publishers, editors, photographers and readers. The festival takes place on the campus of The Banff Centre, Canada's leading international learning centre dedicated to creativity, career development and lifelong learning for leading professional artists and managers.

Featuring guest speakers, seminars, book signings, a book fair and readings, the festival offers a wide spectrum of experiences for the participants and the audiences. The highlight of the festival is the presentation of the awards for the international competition. Awards are presented to the best entries in the categories of grand prize, nonfiction, mountain culture and environment, guide books, mountain images and adventure travel writing.

The finalists for the festival have been selected from over 80 books submitted from six countries. Canadian Bart Robinson, American Allen Steck, Briton Audrey Salkeld and Italian Giorgio Daidola, the final jury for the competition, will select winners in six categories. The jury members are chosen because of their own expertise in the mountain writing field. Daidola is editor of *Rivista della Montagna,* Robinson is the past editor of *Equinox Magazine,* Salkeld is a noted author and Steck is an author and founding editor of *Ascent.*

We have selected excerpts from the following finalists:

- ✓ *Stone Crusade: A Historical Guide to Bouldering in America* by John Sherman
- ✓ *The Game of Mountain and Chance* by Anne Sauvy
- ✓ *Errant Journeys* by David Zurick
- ✓ *Cool of the Wild* by Howard Tomb
- ✓ *Summits & Icefields* by Chic Scott

Stone Crusade

Stone Crusade: A Historical Guide to Bouldering in America
by John Sherman
EXCERPT (PAGE 277)—1990S AND BEYOND
ISBN 0-930410-657-2 292pp
United States: The American Alpine Club; (303) 384-0110

1990s and beyond

by John Sherman

In the early 1990s American bouldering has experienced an explosion of popularity. One of the great things about the sport now is that the medium has remained the same. Sometimes the ground erodes down, or a hold will be missing, but for the most part America's boulderfields have not changed since the inception of the sport. Styles change, techniques evolve, and technology improves, but the boulders remain constant—the one thread that ties all boulderers together.

It is an exciting time to be an American boulderer. Every day it seems another last great problem falls, only to be replaced by something even more outrageous. There are any number of talented boulderers who can do the hardest problems on a given day. It is hard to imagine that today's test pieces will become tomorrow's warm-ups, but it will happen. Only with a sense of history can we put things into perspective. If it were not for the accomplishments of previous generations we would not be where we are today. Our generation has the responsibility of taking the sport forward—discovering new areas, creating new techniques, raising the standards, and providing the next generation with a foundation on which they can build. We are fortunate to have such incredible potential to develop—it is up to us to develop it in good style. We must leave the boulders as nature left them for us, so that the challenge is the same for those in the future as it was for us and those in the past. The future looks bright if we can handle the twin threats of hold-doctoring and loss of access.

Hold doctoring, chiseling, comfortizing, or whatever you want to call it, is nothing new; nevertheless, it is becoming all too commonplace these days. Part of this may be attributed to the advent of climbing gyms, where if you don't like a problem, you just change it. The hold doctors are hacking away at the foundation of the sport—the last great problems they are ruining are only there because previous generations of boulderers were big enough to admit defeat, and generous enough to leave futuristic routes for the next generation.

All important is the concept of bringing ourselves *up* to the level of a problem, not bringing it *down* to our level. It is simply a matter of allowing nature to dictate the challenge. If you don't like the problem, find another. If it is too hard, come back when you are better. If you need to create a challenge, visit gyms.

Peer-group pressure is the best way to discourage chiseling. If you catch somebody doctoring a hold, run them out of town. Chastise them in public. Be merciless: They are stealing from you and the generations to come.

Access is the biggest problem facing the climbing world, and bouldering areas are no exception. Half-a-dozen areas slated for coverage in this book were closed before it went to press. Over half the areas in this book have either been closed in the past or have been threatened with closure. Boulderers must prove themselves to be a worthy and conscientious user group. Removing fixed carpets and minimizing the use of tick marks are two easy steps in the right direction. Turn down the boom box. A little thought for other user groups goes a long ways. Join the Access Fund; join the American Alpine Club.

Another change we are seeing in the 1990s is the introduction of professionalism into bouldering. So far this is a European phenomenon and has only affected a few American areas. A lot of press has been devoted to the accomplishments of Europeans on American boulders lately, giving an unbalanced view of what is going on here. Americans are cranking hard as well, but because they cannot make a living off bouldering, they do not have the incentive to beat their chests in the press. Column inches are currency in the sponsorship game, and the European hotshots know this. If they want to remain sponsored, they have to get their name in print every chance they get.

Eventually, some American climbers may actually make a living from just bouldering, but don't hold your breath. In America the money isn't there yet. When it gets here, achieving sponsorship will be the top goal for some boulderers. Most of these individuals will come and go quickly. Their accomplishments will demand notice, like a colorful bug exploding on a windshield, but, like the bug, they will be washed off at the next fill-up, only to be followed by more of the same.

John Gill once said, "If there is nothing more to climbing than being the best-trained jock, then it is merely gymnastics, a physical abstraction in a narcissistic environment." The world of ratings and magazine headlines is just a glitzy yet flimsy shell hiding the true soul of the sport. The most incredible accomplishments in bouldering have come not from climbers chasing a number, but from climbers chasing a vision.

The Game of Mountain and Chance

The Game of Mountain and Chance **by Anne Souvy**
EXCERPT (PAGE 75)—THE VETERAN
ISBN 1-898573-15-8 £8.99 271pp
United Kingdom: Baton Wicks Publishers, London; (1260) 252963
France: Presses Universitaires de Grenoble, 1995

The Veteran

by Anne Sauvy

The two climbers emerged on the crest, greeted by a violent gust of wind and a flurry of spindrift. Maurice Troènaz, the guide, immediately began to shorten the rope, making several coils which he slid over his rucksack, whilst Léon Puidoux, his client, sitting back on his heels, lost himself in contemplation of the slopes of the North Face of the Gran Paradiso which the two had just climbed together.

One hour later the two men reached the summit of the Gran Paradiso, a long rocky belvedere flanked by curious turrets, which rears up like a vessel's prow between the valleys of Cogne and Valsavaranche. Clouds filled the low-lying plains, and only the snowy mountain ranges rose up into the sun, like golden islands floating on a sea of luminous vapour.

A statue of the Virgin crowns the summit. The pair settled down on a large stony platform nearby.

'There is nothing to the descent,' said Maurice, reassuringly. "A beginner in Class 6 could do it on skis. It's a glorious day, and we're not in any hurry now. Take as many photos as you like. But let's have a bite first. It's nearly eleven hours since we left the hut, though it may not feel like it, and we've had practically nothing to eat. All the same, I'd have expected better conditions at this time of year. But we've done well, and it's not too late.'

'That last six ropelengths on hard ice, where you had to cut steps all the way,' replied Monsieur Puidoux, 'I don't think I've come across any ice like that since the North Face of the Ebnefluh. Have some sausage? Here, let me give you a piece of bread. Where's the thermos?...Sorry, I'll have a quick sip first; my throat's like blotting-paper. Whew, that's better! Here, your turn! And the belays weren't too great, either, with all the ice you kept knocking down on me. Cold, too...my fingertips went completely numb, which rarely happens to me. My hands were quite dead by the time I came to remove the belay screws and move on. Where's that cheese got to? I'm sure there's a bit left...ah, here it is. What some? The séracs were solid, and we were lucky to find those ribs of hard snow the whole way up the first part! We lost a lot of time at that second bergschrund. I really enjoyed it! A good climb, excellent!'

All the parties which had come up by the normal route had already got to the top and gone down again. All except one, which at last slowly reached the crest and forced its way across the rocky outcrops on the summit ridge. The leader was Franco Revel, a Courmayeur guide whom Troènaz knew well, and whom he had greeted the evening before, at the hut. His client was at the end of his tether. He was a tall, clean-shaven old man whose white hair fluttered in the mountain wind. His face bore the signs of exhaustion. He let himself sink to the ground by the side of the statue, and, resting his head against it, shut his eyes and tried to get his breath back. Revel took a thermos flask from his rucksack and make him drink a mug of hot liquid.

'*Va bene*,' said the tourist. '*Ho bisogno solamente di riposarmi un poco...Non preoccuparti.*'

The guide did his best to wedge him firmly, using his rucksack and, unroping, he went to joint the others who were a few metres away, giving them a meaning look.

'What's the matter with him?' asked Troènaz.

'Nothing except old age,' sighed Franco, lighting a cigarette. 'Old age and the obstinacy of a mule. He's one of my clients from Milan, he's been climbing with me for a long time. But he's not up to it any more, he's past it. To think he wants to do Mont Blanc again, at seventy. What a hope. It's quite something that he got as far as this. But he reckons this is just a training climb. Once we're down I'm going to have a tough job getting him to admit he has to give up the high mountains. And other climbing too, most likely. You can see how he feels. Mountains were his life; he doesn't have many other interest. His wife died young, his children aren't very pleasant to him, and he owns a small factory which is causing him anxiety. It'll be a terrible wrench for him, giving up the mountains. Still...there's a time for everything, isn't there?

'Sure,' replied Maurice Troènaz.

'Well, good to have seen you again,' said Revel, throwing away his bag-end. "I'd better go back to the old boy. We're not down yet. See you at the Guides' Festival on 15th August. I'll be coming with the Courmayeur delegation. We'll have a couple of jars. 'Bye, Maurice.'

'See you, Franco! Good luck for the descent.'

Monsieur Puidoux had been listening to the conversation without saying a word. From time to time he glanced at the statue and the elderly, dried-up figure leaning against it. He went on automatically chewing bread and slices of sausage, without going over the memories of the recent climb as he normally did.

Suddenly, sounding somewhat portentous, he called to his guide.

'Maurice,' he said, 'I want you to make me a solemn promise.'

Troènaz stared at him in surprise, about to laugh, but

Léon Puidoux's expression was grave.

'I'm not joking, Maurice. I'm going to ask you to swear an oath. You must sweat you will never let me get like that...that...

He hesitated a moment, searching for words.

'That old wreck,' he finally went on. 'That bit of human scrap...that caricature of a mountaineer. Never let me get to be a shadow of myself...Never let me labour up easy slopes, panting, because I didn't know when to stop climbing...I'm sure this poor fellow has no idea what's happened to him, or he'd feel ashamed. As for what that Italian guide said, it's true, there really is a time for everything, and you have to be able to admit it, have the sense to stop in time. So this is what I'm asking you, Maurice: I'm asking you to tell me the truth before I reach that stage. Mind you, I'm pretty sure I'll notice for myself, but you never know, it may come on imperceptibly, and I want to go out honourably, before I get like...like him.'

'But you're miles away from that!' exclaimed Maurice. 'You've just done the North Face of the Gran Paradiso in fine style. A youngster couldn't have done it better. Sure on your feet, sound in wind and limb, the lot! Hell, it's a real pleasure to see you cramponning. How old are you anyway? Fifty-six? Fifty-seven? OK, fifty-seven. You've got many good years ahead of you. And good climbs, too.'

Léon Puidoux's face lit up. Of course, he knew perfectly well he'd been climbing like a youngster this mourning. But even if you stay healthy and fit, you can't ignore the stealthy accumulation of the years, the verdict of successive calendars, the poignant approach of the final reckoning. Léon Puidoux frequently thought about it. It seemed to him only yesterday that he'd celebrated his fiftieth birthday with a good party, and so as to have the company of all his friends he'd even paid for Maurice to come along with his father, Auguste Troènaz, who had been his first guide, was now retired, and to tell the truth was hardly older than Puidoux himself.

'Of course I know it's not going to be immediately,' he said. 'Moreover, I can say that so far as I'm concerned everything's fine. I get on very well with my wife. She's always right behind me, and with my three sons, not to mention my wonderful granddaughter. My professional work is satisfying too. And though I won't claim I'd say goodbye to the mountains with a light heart, I believe I'll be able to accept it when the time comes, and there'll be many other things to interest me in life, thank God. But I am absolutely determined never to make such a spectacle of myself as that poor pig-headed old man we've just met. So Maurice, that's why I'm asking you - asking you most earnestly - to swear you'll tell me the moment you see me showing real signs of decline, just in case I don't notice myself.'

'But, look here,' objected Maurice embarrassed.

'Sorry, I must insist,' went on Léon Puidoux. 'I beg you. It's a service I'm asking you to do me, as a friend, and it means a lot to me. Promise, or I shall feel this beautiful day has been spoilt.'

'O.K.—Don't worry. If it means so much to you, then I give you my word,' agreed Maurice Troènaz. 'But I don't expect to have to keep my promise in a hurry, I can tell you.'

Léon Puidoux smiled happily. Relieved of his anxiety, he now wanted nothing but to revel in the sense of contentment induced by this latest climb, this additional north face, this new summit. He amused himself by identifying the peaks and ranges which rose up from the blanket of cloud, pulled out his old Rollei to click away at the landscape, and when, wanting to be photographed himself, he gave the camera to Maurice, the latter had to suppress a little smile when he noticed the effort his client was making to stand up straight and saw him smooth several strands of hair over his balding brow with an apparently casual gesture.

A few moments later, on the descent, Troënaz's rope caught up with Franco Revel's. Revel's client, clearly exhausted, was moving like an automaton, taking small and cautious steps. Léon Puidoux lengthened his stride to overtake him, even though the snow was already deep and soft away from the track.

'At this rate they won't get to the hut before evening,' he muttered, for the benefit of his guide.

Maurice Troënaz had been right in assuring Monsieur Puidoux that his fitness and experience would allow him to go on climbing for many more years. In following seasons their partnership was successful in making some very fine expeditions which included the Route Major, the East Ridge of the Crocodile, the Pilier Cordier, the Dent Blanche and the South Face of the Meije. Monsieur Puidoux trained regularly during the year and, when he arrived in Chamonix, he was almost ready to attack big climbs straight away. He had only a very slight tendency to harp on the fact that he was not feeling the ravages of age.

'I feel really on form these days,' he would announce. 'I hope it doesn't sound boastful, but I don't see myself growing old. This winter I went cycling every Sunday. My sons don't do as much. And at Fontainebleu I can still do the same circuits, and even occasionally a new problem. I feel really young, and that's a fact. Do you know, Maurice, if the light's good I can still read *Le Monde* without glasses!'

Maurice Troënaz, who had no intention of reading *Le Monde*, with or without glasses, nevertheless greeted the announcement of this feat deferentially.

'And you won't forget your promise, will you?' Léon Puidoux reminded him from time to time, usually when they had returned from a good climb. You know what I mean. The promise you made on the Gran Paradiso, to warm me when I start going downhill.'

And his guide would invariably and obligingly reply, 'Well, that won't happen in a hurry.'

Several years went by in this fashion until one day, quite suddenly, after a week's holiday during which they had already successfully done two good routes, a phone call summoned Léon Puidoux back to Paris on business. He was disconsolate.

'We'll meet again next year,' he declared. 'And at any rate it'll give me the chance to do plenty of skiing this winter. I'm just thinking, though...maybe we could get round to doing the Chamonix/Zermatt traverse we've talked about so much during our last week? I've never managed to find time for it yet.'

Unfortunately, a nasty fall off-piste at Val-d'Isère led to yet another postponement of this plan. Léon puidoux had injured his right knee. There was talk of an operation, and then they tried electrical treatment, to avoid too long a period of immobilization. The knee did not mend well. In May surgery became inevitable, and there could be no question of planning a season's climbing in the summer. Monsieur Puidoux took the opportunity to spend his holidays in the Midi with all his family, but he missed the mountains so much that he went to Chamonix for three days in August to see the Aiguilles again, contact his guide and make plans for next year. He was still walking with a stick, but rested, relaxed and sunburnt, he appeared full of energy. He invited Troènaz to dinner at the Hotel Eden and regaled him at length with his tales of kneecaps and menisci.

'Just one of those accidents bound to happen to a sportsman,' he declared cheerfully. 'In spite of all the time I've had to spend flat on my back, I haven't put on an ounce. I was even able to take an old pair of flannel bags I've had since I was young to the Midi with me. Not an ounce. I've never felt so fit in my life."

All the same, next summer Maurice saw that Léon

Puidoux had changed. A year's stressful work had left him tired. His firm was facing a multitude of problems. The accounts did not balance, and foreign companies, being more competitive, got the contracts. There was talk of laying off some of the staff. Throughout the year Léon Puidoux had to battle on in difficult conditions, taking home his files in the evenings and over the weekend, and he had almost no time for training. On top of this, the unexpected interruption caused by his accident had somewhat lowered his spirits. His face was gaunt, his hair thinning, and it was evident that he found the mountains harder going than before. On the other hand, he no longer breathed a word about the promise. Maurice sought patiently to reacclimatize him, but the results did not live up to his hope.

'Perhaps it'll be better next summer,' he thought to himself.

But he was never able to tell, because the season was a wash-out. A few climbs in the Aiguilles Rouges and on the Rocher de Leschaux—that was all the two of them managed to snatch from the appalling weather. Once again, major projects had to be postponed for a year.

Eventually they met again the following summer, round the table at the Argentière Hut. Their first climb, to get the legs moving again, was to be the traverse of the Tour Noir, but Maurice Troènaz scrutinized his client with concern. This time the change in him was profound, so much so that the short descent from the Grands Montets téléphérique to the glacier had already tired him out. His heavy lids and the dark marks under his eyes made circles of wrinkles round them, and the beginnings of a double chin showed here and there. His nose seemed pinched, his gaze remained fixed, and a nervous tic made him continually stroke his lips with his fingers, as if he wanted to wipe them. He drank his soup with little noisy gulps, hardly speaking at all, totally preoccupied with himself and with his weariness.

'We'll see how it goes tomorrow,' said Maurice to himself philosophically.

They did indeed. Monsieur Puidoux found innumerable excuses for his slowness. He was no longer used to his boots, which were hurting him. One crampon was too tight and had to be loosened. The rope was over-long, so that he had to hold too many coils. But when the gap had been reduced, the rope turned out to be too short, and didn't allow him to move with his accustomed rhythm. A number of such excuses were proffered, all the way up to the col. And when, on the summit, Maurice Troènaz suggested abandoning the traverse and going down by the ordinary route, he encountered little opposition.

'Maybe you're right, Maurice,' agreed Monsieur Puidoux. 'I can see some clouds which seem to bode no good.'

During the long descent to Lognan which followed, the guide continued to watch his client, and he remembered his promise. What a stupid commitment to have taken on. What an embarrassing mission, far beyond the bounds of his responsibilities. At the same time, he had to admit that Monsieur Puidoux might have been very wise to take such a precaution, for he was evidently unaware of his own condition, and once in the cable-car he immediately began constructing wholly impossible projects. Maurice Troènaz replied evasively and decided to broach the tricky subject as soon as possible. But of course it couldn't be done in the cabin. Nor in the evening, when he was off duty and they met again at the Guides' Bureau. It wasn't something you could very well mention in public. However, having taken his decision Maurice did not want to delay, so he invited his client to have a drink at Melanie's.

'It's on me,' he insisted. 'There's something I have to tell you.'

It wasn't easy. Léon Puidoux seemed to be doing his best to keep the talk to impersonal subjects such as the accident in the Mount Blanc tunnel, last winter's hurricane, the problems of car-parking...

Maurice interrupted him abruptly. 'Monsieur Puidoux! You remember the North Face of the Gran Paradiso?'

"Do I remember? Ah—do I remember...I think I could describe every detail of that pitch where...'

'That's not it, Monsieur Puidoux. I want to talk about the summit, that time when the old Italian arrived utterly knackered. You wrung a promise out of me then. Okay, this is what I have to tell you now, and believe me, I don't enjoy it. But I do think that if you don't want to see yourself deteriorating, it's time you stopped climbing.'

'You must be out of your mind, Maurice,' Léon Puidoux snapped. 'Surely you're not going to pass sentence on me after our very first climb, and after such a long, tedious interval...an unintentional one, as you very well know. My work, my knee, the filthy weather, they all played a part. Now I'm starting again in earnest, and we'll see what we will see. Right, so now I've made that clear, yes, of course I remember the promise I made you give me. And I stick to it, in principle. But I'm amazed, and quite rightly, I really am amazed to find you jumping at the first chance to remind me of it, in such an inopportune way. Unless of course you mean you don't want to climb with me any more and other clients have been monopolizing you over these last few years. In which case, you might have picked some other way of letting me know...'

'No, no, that's not it at all,' stammered Maurice, disconcerted.

'Then we'll forget it' proclaimed Léon Puidoux, in ringing tones. 'You're young, but that's no reason to see me as a relic of mountaineering prehistory. I feel fine, and no matter what you're implying, there aren't many men of my age to equal me, not many at all.'

'But I never said...'

'Maybe not in so many words, but it comes to the same thing. I know what other people are like, and I know myself. I'm glad to say it's not time for me to beat a retreat yet. And please note that when it is time, I'll be able to see it myself, with the clarity of vision I believe I've always shown. In the meantime, I don't think we need to recall the Gran Paradiso. I hope I've made myself quite clear?'

'You certainly have, Monsieur Puidoux,' Maurice agreed.

'Then let's talk about our plans instead,' his client went on mollified. 'I grant you, I do need a bit more training than usual. The rocks are snowed up, but that gives us a chance to do some of the routes I've always dreamt about. 'The Younggrat, for example, I won't suggest the Welzenbach route, also on the Breithorn—you see, I'm being very sensible. On the other hand the Biancograt, on the Piz Bernina, seems a perfectly feasible idea. And then there's the Sentinelle Rouge. I've never yet had any luck there yet. And...'

Maurice Troènaz listened, feeling depressed. He had tried to speak out, and had obviously got nowhere. What more could he do? He steered the discussion towards the subject of training climbs. Once again, Monsieur Puidoux reacted as if he were in the prime of life.

'The North-East Face of the Courtes? The North Buttress of the Charonnet?'

They finally agreed, with some hesitation on both sides, on the Rochefort Ridge. Léon Puidoux found this project too modest, whilst Maurice Troènaz thought it too ambitious, and it was he who was proved right in the end—they had to turn back at the foot of the Dent du Géant, having lost far too much time. They tried two other routes without any greater success. Monsieur Puidoux was in a bad temper, kept finding good reasons to explain his lack of form and complained—although not being successful in getting up anything—of not moving on the Couvercle Hut, where

Maurice recognized Franco Revel at another table and hurried over to greet him.

'Come and have a quick word,' he said. 'I want to ask you a question.'

And when they had moved away from the crowded tables, he said: 'I've been thinking about you lately. I was wondering what happened to your client, the one on the Gran Paradiso. You remember, the day you were with that old man who didn't want to pack it in.'

'You bet I remember,' replied Revel. 'Poor old boy, I guess he must be dead. Anyway, he doesn't write to me any more. It was a tough job, getting him to see he had to call it a day.'

'Exactly!' Maurice persisted. 'Just how did you do it? You see I've got the same problem. We'd done the North Face that day on the Gran Paradiso. Well, up on the summit, when my client saw yours he made me promise never to let him get to that point. And now he's not far from it, I just can't make him understand.'

'You told him, then? Franco asked, with some interest.

'Yes, I told him. He made me promise, after all.'

And Troènaz described what he had done in detail.

'You used words to tell him,' said Franco. 'Now you must try another way, without words.'

'So how do you expect me to tell him except in words?'

'Another way, I said. Or rather, the mountain must tell him. How did you react to his plans?'

'Well, I'm doing my best to make him slow down, show him he can't do these things any more.'

'And he objects, right?'

'You've said it, he most certainly does object. There's no end to the argument. But he just isn't up to it anymore, even on the easy routes. And he's not happy about it either.'

'Well, you can at least make him happy,' suggested Franco. 'Go along with his suggestions and then, like I said, the mountain will do the job itself. It may be a harder way in the end, but I can't see any other.'

'I guess you're right,' Maurice decided.

Next day, Monsieur Puidoux walked for only an hour, towards the Pointe Isabelle. The slopes seemed tedious to him, leading to a boring objective which didn't even provide a genuine high-altitude training.

'But what would you have preferred? Troènaz asked, once they were back in the valley.

'Oh, I don't really know...something different, anything, A real training climb up to 4000 metres, before tackling the serious stuff. Never mind these hills with their cattle pastures where you're getting me into training—why don't we try a big one, Monte Rosa, say? And once I'm used to the altitude again, then depending on the conditions I'm thinking of a route like the Biancograt, or maybe the Zmutt ridge. And after that..'

'Right,' replied Maurice. 'We'll leave for Zermatt tomorrow, if you like, and do Monte Rosa. Whatever you say. I want you to enjoy yourself.'

Surprised by his rapid victory, Léon Puidoux displayed no wild enthusiasm. 'You've certainly taken your time to get the idea,' he remarked tersely.

Maurice Troènaz prepared the climb with care. If the mountain was to speak, as Revel had said it would, he might as well try to smooth the rough side of its tongue. The message was likely to be outspoken anyway. Besides, more than one such occasion might be needed to drive the point home. Maurice had made up his mind that for his part he would display the utmost patience.

They could not leave as soon as they had intended, since they had to wait for a depression accompanied by frequent downpours to pass over, so Monsieur Puidoux felt quite rested when the two men reached Zermatt. He was in a very talkative mood. The Bétemps Hut, two hours away from

Rotenboden station took the two of them in along with quite a number of other people intending to do the climb. A positively military discipline reigned in the hut: those climbers who were aiming for the North Face of the Lyskamm, and wanted to leave before the Monte Rosa mob, found themselves put firmly in their place. Departure time was the same for everybody, and the warden made a point of locking the door for the night. Troènaz felt sorry: he would gladly have joined the Lyskamm climbers to get a head start and gain time in the morning.

Sure enough next morning Monsieur Puidoux and his guide very soon found themselves at the tail end of the procession strung out on the slopes, and although they were not the only ones to be slow, they kept on losing ground. Maurice was determined to remain entirely passive. Too bad if they were outstripped by all and sundry. They went at Monsieur Puidoux's pace, stopped whenever he wanted to stop, started again only when he said he was ready to start, and—above all—there was no looking at watches. They were going to take their time, all the time they wanted..

The highest point of Monte Rosa has an altitude of 4634 metres, but the Bétemps Hut is only at 2800 metres, so you have to climb a height difference of over eighteen hundred metres, along interminable snowslopes. There are no appreciable technical difficulties, except for a few enormous crevasses which have to be circumvented or crossed on snow bridges. Otherwise, it's just a matter of following the deep track which leads to the summit in some six or seven hours, at a normal walking pace.

But when the first parties were beginning to come down on the way back, Maurice Troènaz and Léon Puidoux were only halfway up. Sitting on his rucksack, Monsieur Puidoux pretended not to notice them. He was absorbed in straightening out a crampon strap, and seemed to pay no attention to the comings and goings on the mountain.

'Shall we go?' Maurice finally asked.

They went, taking small steps. The Swiss guides returning to the hut glanced, with some surprise, at the Chamonix guide lagging so far behind, but there you are—these French make out they can do anything and then they take all day for Monte Rosa, where you don't often see them anyway, busy as they are pottering about near the cable-cars. As for Léon Puidoux, he was slightly surprised that, contrary to his usual custom, his guide did not urge him on, or indeed decide that, at this late hour, it was time to pack it in. Not at all. Troènaz seemed quite resigned to the long haul and was most attentive. He had only to carry on. Since for once he'd got his way over the choice of route. Léon Puidoux wasn't going to have it all end in failure. It would just take a bit of time, that's all. He was going to show that he was up to it. But he didn't feel too good. His heart seemed to be beating in his throat. Every five or six paces he felt so breathless that he had a short fit of dry coughing. And there seemed to be two little dazzling, luminous ventilators at the back of his eyes, clouding his vision.

There was no denying that this climb was becoming a real torment. The crevasses were opening up, and the snow bridges were no longer very firm. One of them, a kind of yellowish plug, split in the middle made Monsieur Puidoux freeze in his tracks.

'I managed to get across it, and I've got you on a tight rope,' urged Maurice. 'Come on, then. We're lucky the bridge is still here at this time of day, after all those hordes have trampled across.'

They had reached 4000 metres, and it was already half past ten. Bright clouds were drifting in a dark blue sky, but there was not the slightest breath of wind and the heat was intense.

'I feel so hot,' sighed Léon Puidoux.

'Well, if the wind was blowing, as it often is up here, you'd be complaining of the cold. You know what the mountains are like.'

'I feel hot,' repeated Léon Puidoux.

They took four hours to get up the last six hundred metres, frequently stopping for a rest. The ridge at the end, studded with rocks, cost the old man a quite disproportionate effort. Troènaz said nothing and showed exceptional forbearance. He did not say a word about the way time was getting on, and just kept a bit of tension on the rope to help his client make progress.

On the summit Monsieur Puidoux collapsed on his rucksack. The guide had trouble making him drink and suck a few sweets.

'I think the mountains are changing,' muttered the old man, as if to excuse himself. 'It must be the extra glaciation, or maybe there's less glaciation.'

'That's right,' said Maurice. 'The mountains are changing, the crevasses have got deeper and the slopes even steeper since last time. And I don't know if you've noticed, but the days aren't the same as they sued to be either, probably because of summer time. It's nearly half past two. Makes you wonder where the time has gone. We're the only ones who don't change, see? Here, make a bit of an effort, try to eat that marzipan bar.'

'Leave me alone, Maurice' begged Monsieur Puidoux. 'I'm really not hungry. I just need some rest.'

'Well, you've done Monte Rosa now,' continued Maurice, who was afraid that the old man might fall asleep. 'You were right, after all, and now we must think about the Biancograt...'

But Monsieur Puidoux was hardly listening. He was thinking that he still had to go back down those endless snow slopes he has just toiled up, and the prospect was shattering. For a moment he dreamt of a helicopter... suppose he could be picked up here. He'd be willing to pay all that was required, and more...But how could he let them know down below? How could he even admit it to Maurice? It would be the most abject surrender imaginable. No, he knew very well that he had to make the descent on foot, cost what it might.

It was an immense effort just to stand up. But he managed it and, firmly held on a tight rope by Maurice, who remained amazingly calm, he tackled the start of the descent step by step, move by move, his legs seeming to tuck into his body. So many folds and ridges in the ground, slopes, hollows, detours, crevasses to be skirted or jumped. When they reached the one which had given them so much trouble on the way up, the bridge had collapsed and they would have to make a considerable leap to get across.

'I can't do that,' said the old man.

'Of course you can,' replied Maurice. 'And to prove it, you're going to. I'll be holding you.'

'No, it's much too wide...it's quite impossible. Isn't there some way round? Surely there must be.'

'Well, just look at it. You can't see either end. And this still looks the likeliest spot. You'll land right in the middle of the track. Come on, let's get moving. Any idea how late it is? We've jumped plenty of other crevasses together, crevasses just like this one.'

'I can't do it,' Monsieur Puidoux insisted.

In the end Maurice jumped first and threatened to pull on the rope. His elderly client apprehensive and clumsy, finally took off and crash-landed on the other side in a motionless little heap. In alarm, the guide hastened to bend over him, but there was nothing the matter except fear, exhaustion and shame.

Troènaz could not help giving his companion a bit of a shove, to relieve his feelings.

'Come on, get up. There's nothing the matter with you. Haven't broken you hip, have you? So why all this fuss? Talk about luck.'

The descent continued, even more slowly. The number of rests they took increased. When evening came, they had not yet reached the last zone of crevasses. They had to switch on their head-torches and look for faint traces of a track in the fading light.

'Perhaps we could get a bit of a move on,' muttered Maurice from time to time.

Léon Puidoux was disconcerted by all this forbearance. If he had been sworn at, he would have sought answering arguments, blamed the poor conditions, condemned the equipment, explained that their delay had made the climb longer and therefore more tiring, and so on and so forth, anything. Instead, he was brought face to face with himself, his utter weariness and the vague thoughts which failed to distract him but always homed in on a single goal—to get it over and done with.

It was nearly midnight when they arrived at the upper Plattje rocks where climbing parties unrope, still some way from the hut. Monsieur Puidoux was tottering with fatigue.

'I'm not going to walk another step,' he announced.

'We'd better spend the rest of the night here,' Maurice decided. 'You can't stand upright, and that's a fact. I've had enough myself. I brought some duvet jackets, even a little stove which I carried all the way up, for nothing yet. I'll heat us up some soup. We'll be better off finishing what's left of the descent by daylight.'

They huddled against a rock. The cold, though not intense, was unpleasant. Maurice tried to keep Monsieur Puidoux's morale up by telling him about other, far more uncomfortable bivouacs, and describing the excellent lunch they would have in Zermatt next day. Then, seeing that his client was shivering, he suggested moving on, now they had had a rest, and getting to the hut to spend the rest of the night in the warmth, under good blankets. Monsieur Puidoux did not reply.

'We need to get our strength back, though' Maurice persisted. 'The glaciers are beginning to open up. You saw that today. But the snow's crusted, and it strikes me the Zmutt Ridge should be in good shape. Seeing we're on the spot, why don't we have a good night in Zermatt tomorrow, and then go back up to the Hörnli Hut?'

But there was no response to indicate that Monsieur Puidoux had heard this last proposition.

In the small hours of the morning, the parties going up roused the two men who, when they were alone again, got ready to continue their descent. Despite his long climb yesterday and his uncomfortable night, Monsieur Puidoux seemed to have perked up considerably. After breakfast at the hut, he even set out on the return to Rotenboden with some vigor.

'He hasn't understood a thing,' thought Maurice. 'Good grief! How many trips like this will it take him?'

They settled down at last in the rack-railway and, searching in their rucksacks, instantly created around themselves with their crampons, ice-axes, cagoules and rope that muddle familiar to mountaineers, which the tourists sitting next to them contemplate with mingled disapproval and curiosity. Maurice was aware of the situation and told himself that even this must be hard to leave, the aftermath of a time when you feel different from other people, still being so near that upright world to which they have no access. But Léon Puidoux looked far away from the scene. Huddled into a corner of his seat, he sat gazing straight ahead, his eyes, their irises now paling, fixed on God knows what invisible point. All at once, an age-spotted hand pensively stroking his cheeks, where grey stubble was sprouting, he looked sadly at the guide and then, turning towards the window of the compartment where the Matterhorn was framed, outlined against the blue sky in the glory of the morning, he whispered, very quietly, 'I'm through, Maurice.'

Errant Journeys

Errant Journeys: Adventure Travel in a Modern Age
by David Zurick
EXCERPT (PAGE 130)—PUSHING INTO THE PERIPHERY
ISBN 0-292-79806-7 206pp
United States: University of Texas Press; (512) 471-7233

Pushing into the periphery

by David Zurick

Since the mid-1970s, when trekking became popular in the Himalaya, tourism in Nepal's Annapurna region has made considerable inroads into mountain society and has dramatically altered the mountain landscape. Signboards along the mountain trails announce the Gurkha-run lodges that are found now in many villages scattered across the region, from the valley town of Pokhara to the highland settlement of Ghandruk, which is now the regional center of a new, tourism-based conservation project. On the trekking routes, porters bearing tourist loads regularly pass mule traders hauling salt from faraway Tibet—old practices with a new twist. Village children eagerly greet tourists along the popular trails with rapid-fire cries of candy! rupee! pen! The ingress of tourism into the Annapurna highlands juxtaposes the new commercial economy with older subsistence ones, material affluence with poverty, and secular world views with those that see in the land all the possibilities of God.

Crossing Distances

The high peaks that physically bound the Gurung world delimit also the sacred inner realm of the high country; the Gurungs mark the trails into the mountains with religious shrines to honor the spirits that dwell therein. By thus signing the path, they mark also the journey into the mythic and supernatural worlds of the Gurung. The majestic mountains of Annapurna evoke awe but also humility, render the Gurung universe complete, and the travelers who pass among them enter a moral order that ultimately is unfathomable, as elusive as the chimera of ice and snow on the mountain summits. Such a journey must be mediated by ritual and by ceremony. The Gurungs know this, as do native peoples worldwide, for whom the idea of culture and nature are practically inseparable, and they weave religious observances into the daily fabric of their lives. All over the world, we find, among the old ceremonies and cultural legends, similar markers of the spiritual journey. The ancient grotto paintings of Lascaux, the food taboos of the San Bushman of Africa, the totems of Native Americans living in the Pacific Northwest region of North America, the Navajo sand paintings, Krishna dances in India, the Buddhist *thankas*, the Garden of Eden, all show the storied landscapes that define how one should properly live. And they all point to sacred elements of the physical world which unite people into cultures with supernatural origins.

Such things may be meaningless, however, to the thousands of newcomers who venture into these places as tourists from the modern, secular societies of the Western world. For them, reason rather than myth matters most. Logic, valuable as it may be in solving the puzzles of modern technology, proves less useful when dealing with the larger riddles of human consciousness. Across the world through time, the latter have required mainly spiritual approaches, and for guidance they demand knowing something of the old myths and stories. If contemporary Western society no longer holds a valid myth, as some assert, then that may be why people search other cultures—to discover that which may be lost in their own.

I often meet trekkers who go into the Himalaya regions purposefully to undertake the elements of a mythic journey, much as the overland travelers do in a more prolonged fashion. They attempt an abridged version of a mystic quest and see in their mountain trek the opportunity to quickly attain the main elements of a mythical journey: the *departure,* crossing the threshold into the imagined but still unknown places, the *initiation,* personal or spiritual anointments that require ritual and supernatural assistance, the *return,* the conquest of self, the completed quest, and the coming of the hero.

In seeking out the high Himalaya, such trailers look for the *axis mundi,* the center point of the world which figuratively and symbolically may exist in the landscape—certainly for the Hindus and the Buddhists the mountains are that, especially Mount Kalash (but so is Harney Peak in South Dakota for the Sioux); ultimately, of course, it is found only within. As I remember my own companionship in such experiences, my recollections of the Annapurna trails are of making my way through blazing rhododendron forests, scrambling dangerously across frozen waterfalls, meeting a shaman in the woods whose presence was as ephemeral as the jasmine blossoms that flowered along the icy trail and finding relief among the stone-and-timber huts of a village.

The many-layered half-memories of countless similar journeys take the shifting form of a fantasy, and I am reminded of the stories of British author J.R.R. Tolkien. His books, especially *The Hobbit* and *the Lord of the Rings* (a three-volume trilogy), masterfully catch the light and the shadow of a journey in Nepal: indeed they are to be found among the most precious possessions of many stripped-down mountain trekkers, precisely because they weave tails as fanciful as the experiences tourists are likely to obtain in such a place as the Annapurna mountains. So alike are the peaks, the forests, and the villages of Nepal to the fantastic landscapes of Tolkien, so common are the characters that resemble the cast of those stories—the Gandalfs and Gollums and the "keepers of the inns by the side of the road"—that many travelers, without apparent validation, believe that Tolkien had once lived there, especially at a forested place called Ghorapani, when he conceived those remarkable stories. Like the shrines that the Gurungs place at the entries to their sacred mountain realm, passages from Tolkien's books ("...and the road goes forever on...") inscribe the tourist landscapes, are found in the lodge ledgers, on restaurant walks, in numerous journals, such that they too become markers into a mystical landscape. The books simultaneously validate travelers impulses and allow them to escape the often deplorable conditions at hand, when reality fails miserably to match the fantasy. The books are more than escapist literature, although that is how they may appear on the booksellers' shelves, but instead compose the structure and the motifs of a serious life journey.

When adventure tourists push at the perimeter of the world, they are doing more than connecting financial institutions or establishing other social linkages. They are entangling Western and non-Western concepts of life into an emerging image of a united world. This is the view we can gain from satellite glimpses of the earth, where political lines dissolve into great circulations of water, land, and air. A new mythology, one that connects distant places and peoples into a comprehensive and shared story of the past and the future, is implied by the participation of tourists on an adventure itinerary and rendered explicit in their creation by the adventure agencies.

Cool of the Wild

by Howard Tomb

***Cool of the Wild* by Howard Tomb**

EXCERPT (PAGE XI)—THE JOY OF TERROR
ISBN 0-8092-3774-1 USD$10.95 170pp
Canada: Fitzhenry & Whiteside Publishers; (905) 477-9700
United States: Contemporary Books, Chicago

The Joy of Terror

We who live in "developed" societies are up to our ears in static—seemingly random signals that make no sense. As technologies pump even more information at us, our confusion deepens and our worries multiply like cockroaches. We become distracted from what's truly important.

Some of us are able to break out of the modern fog, however. People who survive near-fatal accidents or recover from serious illnesses, for instance, often change their priorities; they have a new appreciation for the untouchable, for the mysterious glories of life. They have a new thirst for beauty and a new distaste for all things petty, mean-spirited, and quotidian. They feel comfortable telling their bosses to suck dogmeat.

Unfortunately, postindustrial chaos overwhelms most of these survivors, and they mix up their priorities and sink back into their worrying, sniveling ways.

A few members of modern society, however, regularly refresh their courage: the wilderness adventurers, the unflappable masters, the cool of the wild. Instead of relying on luck to survive an awful disease or car crash, for example, they hone their skills in one or more dangerous pursuits so they can dance along the brink of disaster regularly and *on purpose*.

Because the cool of the wild keep their priorities straight, they can remain calm when, say, somebody drops the last piece of their favorite lasagna on a filthy kitchen floor. My lasagna has hairs on it now, they might think to themselves, but at least my skull has not been crushed by a falling block of granite.

While a postindustrial person might shout curses, endure a potentially lethal rise in blood pressure, and feed the soiled lasagna to the nearest dog, the master simply accepts the many-layered nature of lasagna, peels away the gritty portion, and enjoys the rest. I have slightly less lasagna now, the master might think, but a twenty-two-foot saltwater crocodile is not tearing my leg off.

Finding this kind of peace and poise in our frenetic world takes practice and dedication, but huge are the rewards. Grace and terror combine in a multitude of forms; this book is meant to help readers achieve them using the more popular and effective methods.

The sports are divided into four general categories: extreme climbing, extreme skiing, extreme wetness, and extreme falling. It's hard to judge which is most insane: jumping off an office building, for example, climbing a wall of ice, or sailing across the Pacific Ocean accompanied only by a small dog. Although all of these flood the bloodstream with Exotic Chemicals of Fear, different sports appeal to different kinds of people. We have provided exclusive Archetype ProFiles to guide you in exploring new avenues of terror and deciding which group of nutbags you'd like to join.

Break a leg.

Extreme Climbing

Making love to granite

Rock climbing is becoming more popular with people who went to Club Med in the 1980s. Bored by luxury and comfort, they now want to strap colorful harnesses tightly around their loins, suffer exquisitely, and have multiple achievements.

Climbers can display wealth and taste in the parking area: dozens of bits of protection at $50 each, new ropes, and outfits, satin chalk bags, $300 sunglasses, whatever. Once they get on a cliff, however, they generally move out of sight and all showing off comes to an end. Most routes are out of sight even to people holding the ropes. This makes rock climbing the ideal antiglamour sport for the nineties. Unobtrusive and inward-turning, it's existential tag-team wrestling. Your Mind, Your Body, and Rock versus Fear, Gravity and Irreversible Spinal Injury.

Lead Climbing

Even the most talented climbers boulder and top-rope to hone their balance, flexibility, and strength. But there comes a time when that talent must be tested.

The earliest climbers in Europe tied handmade ropes around their waists and held the ropes in cracks with chock stones. They are now dead.

Today the principle of lead climbing is the same, except stones have been replaced by metal nuts and chocks slung with rope, webbing, or wire. Camming devices, such as Friends and Camalots, service the same purpose with more flexibility and at much greater expense.

To lead or "free climb," a climber must learn the arcane craft of protection: attaching rings, called *carabiners,* to the cliff with nuts, chocks, stoppers, and so on. The rope, attached to the climber, slides through the carabiners. The belayer sits or stands below, keeping slack out of the rope, ready to hold it tight in the event of a fall.

Leaders thus fall as far past the last piece of protection as they were above it when they lost their grip. From fifteen feet above their last piece of protection, for example, they would fall thirty feet plus the stretch of the rope, another four or five feet.

The T-Factor

Terror may be psychological, but it does a number on your physical body. When your legs start to shake, for example, your footing becomes less secure, and that scares you more. Your hands start to sweat so hard the rock feels slimy. You sense not only that you may peel off the rock but that your sense that you may peel off the rock may actually cause you to peel off the rock.

At this point you turn a mental corner and ask yourself the age-old Adventurer's Question: Why am I here?

Corollaries then spring to mind: (a) Is it really so bad to drink an entire six-pack of beer in a prone position while watching people fish for bass on TV? (b) Is there a God? (c) Might I make a bargain with Him right this second to save my sorry ass just this one time?

Many things can sharpen the T-factor on a rock climb. Height, for example. Any fall onto jagged boulders from over seventy feet is going to be fatal, but the deepest fears are unreasoning fears: most people find seven hundred feet scarier than seventy.

The height above the last protection or lack of confidence in its placement can make a relatively easy move seem impossible.

A climb's reputation can make it more difficult. If you've fallen from it before or it's never been climbed, it may be especially daunting.

Simple tasks can be turned into challenges by countless things: fatigue, a comment your accountant made last week, a really large spider staring at you from a crack, and so on.

We can learn to overcome the T-factor, to accept the fear and work through it, and to forget how it felt so we can put ourselves in new and even more terrifying situations next weekend.

That, in fact, is how bravery is made: practice. The happiest and most successful people have learned to swallow doubt and fear and *make the move.*

People who never exercise their courage get a flabby pluck. When they suddenly need strength to stand up to a human or spiritual enemy, they are easily beaten.

Summits & Icefields

by Chic Scott

***Summits & Icefields* by Chic Scott**

EXCERPT—INTRODUCTION TO THE GRAND TRAVERSES
Canada: Rocky Mountain Books; (403) 249-9490

Western Canada has a number of wilderness ski traverses which cross the ice fields of the Rockies, Selkirks, Purcells, Cariboos and Valhalla. These traverses have been pioneered over the last 40 years and are gradually becoming more and more popular. Some of them are now done every year.

They are major ski adventures, up to 300 km in length, and present the problems of any large expedition. Thankfully, they do not involve the hassles associated with expeditions to foreign lands. The problems to be dealt with here are only those presented by the mountains themselves.

In this section seven of these traverses are described. To begin with there are some general tips on how to successfully complete one of these adventures, then each trip is described in detail complete with a little history and some planning notes specific to each traverse.

Good luck if you attempt one of these 'Grand Traverses.' Do not take them lightly; they are major undertakings. While you do not have to be an expert mountaineer or a super skier to complete a traverse, you must be well organized, experienced and committed.

Equipment

Most everyone who has skied these traverses has used a Nordic-style back country ski with a cable binding and a sturdy pair of backcountry touring boots.

This type of equipment has been found to be lighter than the randonnee skis and plastic boots, but still provides adequate control for the downhills. Remember that you will be skiing with a heavy pack many miles from the highway and getting down the hill safely and cautiously will be the goal, not aggressive turns. In addition, the large majority of the time you are ascending or traversing long icefields and wilderness valleys. Downhill skiing makes up a relatively small percentage of the trip.

Be prepared to deal with winter conditions and temperatures of perhaps minus 20°C. Tents and sleeping bags should be of high quality and should be very comfortable because you may have to wait out bad weather for long periods of time.

Planning

Meticulous planning is the key to a successful expedition. If all your gear functions well, if the food caches are properly placed and if you know the route well, then it is simply a matter of several weeks of enjoyable skiing. Of course, you must have some luck with the weather, but given a normal season you can expect to ski about two days out of three. If you look individually at each day then it's not too difficult. It is just a matter of putting a lot of these days together.

You should study the route in detail beforehand, using maps, air photos and any written reports available. If possible talk to someone who has done the trip. The better you know the route the more confident you will feel and the easier it will all seem. Know your escape routes in the event of an emergency.

Begin planning as early as possible and try to come up with a compatible team of friends. Four is a good number —any less and the trail breaking could be difficult.

Pay great attention to weight of your equipment and try to keep your pack as light as possible. The best time to tackle any of these traverses is late April when the days are long, sunny and warm. However, they have also been successfully completed in both March and May. To a great extent, how late you can travel depends on how heavy the snowfall has been the previous winter. These traverses are definitely not advised in January and February when it is dark, cold and the snow is very powdery.

Beyond the Limits: A Woman's Triumph on Everest

review by Ron Morrow

Beyond the Limits: A Woman's Triumph on Everest
by Stacy Allison with Peter Carlin
Little, Brown and Company
1993. 282 pages

When she was interviewed for an Everest expedition, Stacy Allison was asked a straight forward question. She was asked why she felt that she should be included. She thought for a moment then blurted out "Because I am a nice person" Fortunately, her loss for words was temporary and she was accepted. The rest is history. She became the first American woman to climb Everest. Like so many climbers before her, she wrote a book about her experiences. Her book is also about domestic abuse.

Before Everest, Stacy was a member of Arlene Blum's all-woman expedition to Annapurna. She descended the steep slopes of that mountain to find her fiancee waiting for her. The Sherpas invited the young couple to their village and a traditional Sherpa wedding followed. The entire expedition attended. Photographs captured the ceremony and a happy, smiling Allison.

After the wedding she followed her husband back to his home in Utah. There she quickly discovered his mood-swings and bad temper. The temper kept asserting itself until things escalated to the point where a fist swung out of the darkness.

Wisely she left him. He followed her, contrite and repentant. Eventually, she agreed to return to Utah with him but only with the condition that they seek professional help. Unfortunately that help was a Mormon psychologist who told her, "..husbands tend to react to the way his wife behaves, so, Stacy, you need to ask yourself, What am I doing to make Mark so angry?" The therapy lasted one month, then the abuse resumed, it resumed in a more subtle form. He started to attack and destroy her self-confidence. Slowly he started to make her feel worthless. He backed away from teaching her a marketable skill. When friends called to propose climbs he refused to let her go. The reality of her life as a climber became a reality from the past. Her life was life with him. Then the violence returned. He blackened her eye, then tried to get to her to stay home the next day, failing that, he persuaded her to tell her friends that she had a work site accident.

This is an ugly picture but what is absolutely riveting about the book is Allison's ability to take an unflinching look at herself. When she looks back at herself deliberately helping him hide his activities she admits the cruelest irony of abuse is that his rages actually in a way made them closer. Secreting the shame required two actors that created complicity; sad but real.

Allison is a coldly honest about climbing as she is about her abusive relationship. She readily admits that climbing is a selfish activity. Her first attempt on Everest failed and she examined her disappointment. She discovered that she had invested too much in the idea that she would be the first American woman to summit Everest and that she was using the climb as a crutch to help her poor self image.

When she returns to the mountain the following year she returned with the basic values of climbing. She does not dismiss the importance of being the first American woman to climb the worlds highest summit but she knows that she is much more concerned about being the first

Stacy Allison on the summit. She rediscovers the sheer joy of climbing. Her description of the hard work of making the summit is very much like Leo Tolstoy describing the harvesting of wheat. That is the necessity of continuing the work until the work is done. Like the rhythm of the scythe she put one foot in front of the other until her work is done.

Tracy climbed her mountain and in doing so returned to herself. The bad marriage ended and the reality of it lost form like a period of depression; it was real, then it was over. The description of this process could have been taken verbatim from Soren Kirkegaard. She had a fear of being herself. Then she returned to herself, and the fear seemed silly. It seems especially silly when the book does not reveal a horrible person. Far from it, the Stacy Allison who is revealed is, in fact, a genuinely "nice person".

It is a damn shame that in the current climate of conservative cant, stories like Stacy's are diminished, if not dismissed out of hand. This is an important story and a fine book. I hope that you read it.

Footprints on the Peaks: Mountaineering in China

Review by Robert Schoene

Footprints on the Peaks: Mountaineering in China
Zhou Zheng and Liu Zhankai
Cloudcap
P.O. Box 27344
Seattle, WA 98125-1844
(206) 365-9192
1995

At the onset, I confess to be biased in this review! In both 1988 and 1989 I had the good fortune of being included (probably as the youthful "load-humper") on a trip with a group of veteran American mountaineers, led by Nick Clinch, to the magnificent and rarely visited peaks near the great river trenches of Asia in the northern Yunan Province, on the eastern border of Tibet. Zhou Zheng, Wang Fuzhou, and Chinese International Sport Travel (CIST) were our gracious hosts and facilitators to the alluring peak, Kangkarpo, personal experiences from which led to two of my poems in *The Climbing Art.* It is, therefore, with warmth, especially for Zhou Zheng, that I offer my thoughts on this remarkable book, *Footprints on the Peaks.*

Footprints evolved from a number of years of encouragement and multinational collaboration. The spirit of the book is anchored in the fellowship of mountaineering which if carried into other spheres of life, says Zhou Zheng in the Preface, "would make this world of ours a much better place to live." Although one could quibble about some inaccuracies, deletions, oversights, and some painfully short synopses, this book occupies an important and unique place in mountaineering literature. The book is replete with the sense of historic perspective, reverence for the visionary and poetic, and respect of those who have gone before. Reading it left me breathless and "hypoxic" as I daydreamed about the vast, unexplored mountains which crisscross China and Tibet.

The treasure of this book lies in the recounting of mountaineering in China before the modern era at which times these mountains were opened up for climbing and exploration from the "outside." In fact, more thorough and perhaps accurate accounts of climbing in the years following China's open-door policy in the 1970s are available elsewhere in the world's mountaineering literature. But little is know about exploration and climbing before this time.

Liu Zhenkai wrote the first sections of the book, which deal with mountain geography, early climbing and exploration, and the history of warfare and trade routes. This portion of the book is fascinating and conjures up fantasies of the Silk Route, sacred mountains, poet-climbers, holy men, Marco Polo, and ageless reverence for the magic that the high peaks brew in the minds of men. He covers the Early Period (before 743 A.D.) when descriptions of ropes, altitude illness, and exploration of the Karakorum, Tianshan, Kunlun, and Pamirs Ranges were first made. The hand-drawn maps in this section would benefit from sketching the ranges themselves so as to make history come to life for those of us not familiar with the vast tracts of land which make up all of China and Tibet.

The Middle Period (743-1955 A.D.) starts with the description of the Qinling Mountains and the wanderings of the peripatetic and prolific poet, Li Bai. "Difficult is the road to Shu,/more so than the road/to the heavens blue." The mountains were also appreciated for more than their adventure. Early discovery of the flora and fauna emanate from these early years.

The transition into the modern era, most of which is

undertaken by Zhou Zheng, really begins with the 1932 American ascent of the spectacular 7587-meter peak, Minya Konka or Mt. Gongga (Young, Moore, Burdsall, Emmons). The heart of modern mountaineering by the Chinese and the Tibetans followed between 1955 and the 1970s when China and Tibet were opened to foreigners. Joint Sino-Soviet climbs to the 7000-meter peaks, the still-disputed climb of Everest in 1960, rigorous training, disasters and deaths, the aluminum tripod placed on the summit of Everest in 1975, Shishibangma—all these tales are compellingly told and combine to establish a strong foundation for mountaineering in one of the world's largest and most heterogeneous countries.

The most enchanting story though is the romance between Deng Jiashan from eastern China and Panduo from Tibet who fell in love in 1961 while roped together on Kongur Tibuie. After a dozen years of marriage and children. Deng encouraged Panduo to start training again, which in 1975 led to her becoming the second woman to climb Everest.

There is little politics in the book except Zheng's clear feelings about the Cultural Revolution ("Mountaineering activities had been halted with the outbreak of the disastrous 'Cultural Revolution' in 1966.") Interestingly, the book is illustrated with plates mostly from photographers from outside China. In spite of some of its shortcomings, this book is a gem in and of itself, and as Zhenkai says in the postscript: "No doubt a better one (book) will appear at some future date. Then, and only then, will Zhou and I happily deem our goal fulfilled. For, after all, we are but 'casting a brick to draw out a piece of jade.'"

Contributors' notes

Richard Bennett is a contractor and free-lance writer who now lives on an island in Puget Sound, from where he can see the Olympics and Cascades.

Kathryn de Leon is an elementary school teacher living in Whittier, California. She has been writing poetry for more years than she cares to admit, and she has recently been working on a number or short stories.

Elizabeth N. Evasdaughter grew up in the Osage Hills and has spent a considerable amount of time hiking in the Rockies. She has a book coming out in spring 1996, *Impossible Autobiographers: Catholic Women of the Twentieth Century* (Northeastern University Press), which could be said metaphorically to describe a situation in which a girl is trying to climb a mountain and various officials keep trying to prevent her.

Gary Every, a native of Tucson, Arizona, is employed at the Arizona Sonora Desert Museum. His poetry appears irregularly in *South Ash Press* and *Atom Mind*. His articles have appeared in magazines such as *Desert Skies* and *Desert Ear*.

Terry Gifford is director of annual International Festival of Mountaineering Literature at Bretton Hall College, England. He is author of three collections of poems and contributor to *Ascent '93*.

Chris Hoffman is a poet of the earth-and-spirit tradition. He has recently been published in *Sea Kayaker* magazine and has written lyrics recorded by Monkey Siren. He works as a counselor and consultant, with special interest in ecopsychology.

Susan Jessup is working on a Bachelor's degree in biomedical illustration at Iowa State University. She hails from Seattle where she spends time with her annoying little dog. She hopes to some day illustrate covers for science fiction novels.

Clair Killen was born in 1920 and lived most of his life in southern California. His career has been eclectic. He began writing after attending a writer's workshop with Lawson Inada in the summer of 1993.

Louis Komjathy lives in Seattle where he practices and studies the movements within Taoist tradition. Numerous poems and stories of his have been published , and a collection of poems entitled Alluvial Fans received the Burkehardt Prize in Literature from the University of California, San Diego.

J.J. McKenna happily spends about a month each summer in the Colorado Rockies hiking in the Alpine sone of wilderness areas. His poems have recently appeared in *The Louisville Review, Great Plains Quarterly, Petroglyph, Hawaii Review, Athelon, Kentucky Literary Journal, Eureka Literary Magazine,* and *Voices International.*

Ron Morrow is a firefighter in Denver and co-organizer of the 1997 Firefighters on Everest expedition. He is a Contributing Editor for *The Climbing Art* and an Editor for *The American Alpine News* of the American Alpine Club.

T.R. Petersen considers Puget Sound and the San Juan Islands his home. He lives in Flagstaff, though, where he is pursuing a master's degree in the creative writing program at Northern Arizona University. He is the managing editor of *Thin Air* magazine. His work has appeared in Timberline literary magazine, and he was a participating poet in the 1993 Washington State Poetry Festival.

Robert Schoene is an associate professor at the University of Washington School of Medicine where he is a pulmonary and critical care specialist. He has had the good fortune of being able to combine his research career in high altitude physiology with his passion for high places around the world, including China.

John Svenson is a painter living in Alaska. His mountaineering exploits and travels are frequent subjects of his art.

Tracey Titterington is working an MFA in creative writing at Vermont College. In the mean time she is working for near minimum wage at a rafting company up the Poudre.

Robert Walton has had three children's books published. His short fiction won the John Steinbeck 1st Place Award in 1981 and the Arizona Authors Association Contest 5th Place in 1991. He has stories in Ascent '89 and Ascent '93. He climbs as often as being a father of teenagers allows.

Jim Warren is a mailman who lives in Laguna Niguel, California. He writes and climbs to reach the next level of consciousness. Mountaineering has taken him to Peru, Bolivia, and most recently to Argentina where he spent three memorable days in a tent at 18,000 feet, waiting out the winds of Merdedario.

Paul Willis teaches writing and literature at Westmont College in Santa Barbara, California. He is author of a pair or mountain fantasies: *No Clock in the Forest: An Alpine Tale* and *The Stolen River* (Avon Books). His poems and stories have appeared in *Ascent, Green Fuse* and *Wilderness.*

MOUNTAIN TRIP
Climbing
&
Skiing
Expeditions
For a free brochure
describing Mountain Trip's
professionally guided
expeditions, write:
Mountain Trip
Gary Bocarde
P.O. Box 91161
Anchorage, AK 99509
(907) 345-6499
EXPEDITIONS